DATE DUE

TechnoStress

Dr. Michelle Weil

[signatures]

Coping with Technology
@Work @Home @Play

TechnoStress

MICHELLE M. WEIL, Ph.D.
LARRY D. ROSEN, Ph.D.

John Wiley & Sons, Inc.

New York ‹ Chichester ‹ Weinheim ‹ Brisbane ‹ Singapore ‹ Toronto

Copyright © 1997 by Michelle M. Weil & Larry D. Rosen
Published by John Wiley & Sons, Inc.

Library of Congress Cataloging-in-Publication Data:

Weil, Michelle M.
    TechnoStress : coping with technology @work @home @play / by
  Michelle M. Weil, Larry D. Rosen.
      p.   cm.
    Includes index.
    ISBN 0-471-17709-1 (cloth : alk. paper)
    1. Technology—Social aspects. 2. Technology—Psychological
  aspects. 3. Stress (Psychology) I. Rosen, Larry D. II. Title.
  T14.5.W38   1997
  155.9'1—dc21   97-16114

From MW: This book is dedicated to my best friend, loving husband of many years, playmate, colleague, and soul mate. Thank you for being in my world and helping me be the best I can be, which is so much more than I ever imagined possible.

From LR: Until some greater power brought into my life a wonderful friend and confidant, marvelous co-parent and perfect colleague, I had no earthly idea that I could love, live, and work with one person 24 hours a day and feel challenged, enriched, and loved at every moment. Thank you for being you with me.

Preface

‹ ‹ ‹ ‹ ‹ ‹ ‹ › › › › › › ›

F ifteen years ago we became aware that technology was giving us all a great deal of grief. We have spent many years amassing an undeniable research base to show that the discomfort people are feeling is simply **not** going away and has, in fact, grown to monumental proportions.

Today, there is more technology than ever before. You can't go to the market, get gasoline in your car, or even spend the night in a hotel without encountering countless challenges brought to you by technology. And technology will only continue to infiltrate all our worlds—at work, at home, and at play.

TechnoStress is for everyone. Each of us experiences some degree of stress from technology. Even if we are comfortable with certain technologies, others leave us frustrated, overwhelmed, or feeling downright stupid. Don't you feel a bit apprehensive when you have to learn yet another computer program for work? Doesn't it annoy you when you try to repair a broken appliance only to find that you have to buy a new one that does more than you want or need?

For the millions of people who are not all that comfortable with technology, the daily technological onslaught creates continuing pressure and stress. Do you enjoy having to reset all your digital 12:00, 12:00, 12:00s blinking around the house after a power outage? Do you feel a little left behind by all the www.anothercompany.coms showing up everywhere? Each of us is feeling Techno-Stressed; we are most certainly not alone.

TechnoStress is the irritation we feel as our boundaries are constantly invaded by beeps, pages, and cell phone conversations from the restaurant table next to us at dinner, at the movie theater, or anywhere we previously enjoyed peace and quiet. It is our feeling that we should be able to work as fast as our computers. It is our bewilderment that with so many time-saving devices, we never have enough time. TechnoStress is our feeling of helplessness when our children or neighbors can "surf the Web" and we still do not even know what that means!

TechnoStress addresses these issues and more. This book is about developing a empowered, "winning" attitude about yourself with regard to technology. It is about understanding and overcoming the countless ways you feel frustrated, intimidated, and undermined by the very things that are supposed to make our lives easier.

And *TechnoStress* offers you the solutions. You will come away feeling back in charge of your worlds. No longer will you feel overwhelmed and inadequate—you will feel clear, confident, and self-assured in your knowledge of how to have technology in your life without the stress. We are not antitechnology. Quite the contrary, we are all for technology—but only when it is the right technology for *you*. We believe it is important to develop a belief that **you can master what you want to learn and leave the rest alone.** *TechnoStress* helps you become the driver, not the driven.

Today, many of us are searching for ways to create more meaning in our lives. We long for the feeling of "rightness" about our existence that we seem to have lost along the way, or perhaps never felt at all. We believe the rapid influx of technology has exacerbated this dilemma. In *TechnoStress,* we address these deeper issues and offer clear insight about how to make our life experience more enriched and satisfying.

Enjoy!

Acknowledgments

‹ ‹ ‹ ‹ ‹ ‹ ‹ › › › › › › ›

When a project such as this is finally finished, it is difficult to acknowledge all those of importance without writing yet another entire book! First, we thank the countless technophobes, research subjects, corporations, and colleagues worldwide who have worked with us and helped us build the knowledge base from which we draw. Without you, there would be no book.

We wish to thank our agent, Jody Rein, for believing in this project and believing that we were *the* ones to write it. Jody was willing to "roll up her sleeves" and work very hard with us when necessary. She is a wonderful person to have on our side.

Our editor, Kelly Franklin, has been a believer in us as authors and a firm supporter of this project from its inception. She fought hard to have her "house" get this book, and we were so pleased to be able to work with her on *TechnoStress,* our second book with both John Wiley & Sons and with Kelly as our editor. We have learned a lot about ourselves and about the process of writing a major work from this talented woman.

‹ Acknowledgments ›

We wish to generously thank our family. From our children—Kaylee, Christopher, Arielle, Adam, and Daren—to our parents—Jo, Oscar, and Sarah—your support and encouragement has meant so much. Thanks for all the notes, faxes, flowers, food, e-mails, and calls as we spent countless hours pounding at the keys or were otherwise occupied in this writing process.

A special acknowledgment goes posthumously to Deborah C. Sears, Ph.D., who began in the mid-80s helping us study technophobia in the university. Her untimely, early death still leaves an empty place in us both.

Important recognition goes to MCI Telecommunications Corporation. MCI has been a forerunner in the field as they have continually acknowledged that technology is not easy for everyone! This awareness has led to their cutting-edge attitude in promoting assistance for overcoming TechnoStress in many major projects. We have enjoyed working with them and have met many talented people within their organization. A special note of thanks goes to our dear friend Alf Sauvé. We met Alf through our early work with MCI, and he has become a "necessary ingredient" in our lives. He is there to applaud us, tease us, as well as be incredibly intelligent, all in the right proportion, and with perfect timing. He believes in what we do, in us, and in overcoming TechnoStress.

Contents

‹　‹　‹　‹　‹　‹　‹　›　›　›　›　›　›　›

1

How TechnoStressed Are You?

〈 〈 〈 〈 〈 〈 〈 〉 〉 〉 〉 〉 〉 〉

The alarm clock buzzes, signaling that it is time to get up. In a sleepy haze, you hit the snooze button again and again. Finally, you force yourself out of bed, and the race is on. You're running late. No time for breakfast? Of course there is. The microwave oven will cook it for you while you shower and dress.

A few minutes later, you dash to the car, heading for work. But the gas tank is almost empty and you don't have enough cash to fill up. Not to worry. Pay at the pump with a credit card. And the flurry of activity doesn't end here. There is just enough time to drive to the Automatic Teller Machine (ATM) to replenish your cash on the way to the office.

Now you're ready to start the workday with another familiar routine: check your voice mail, log on to your computer, review the incoming Lotus notes and electronic mail (e-mail) messages. The day has hardly begun and you've already relied heavily on technology to get you going.

We wake up to one electronic device and spend the rest of the day typing on or communicating through others. And when we head home, many of us log on to the Internet, or play interactive video games, or electronically correspond with strangers, friends, and business associates. It seems as though everyone is surfing the Net (or at least they're saying so). And those of us not yet on-line often spend our evenings positioned solidly in front of that familiar technological marvel—the television.

Not many years ago, technology was a novelty, but today it is an integral part of our daily lives, and we can't seem to function without it. We are in the midst of a revolutionary technological shift, the likes of which has never been seen before. But most days, it seems more like a revolutionary war, and we have the battle scars to prove it. The system failure that so often confounds us at work is not just in our computers, it is in us as well.

The proliferation of increasingly sophisticated technology at home and in the workplace has spawned unprecedented use of machines by men, women, and children. Although each individual machine was devised to make our lives easier, or to provide entertainment, collectively the mass of modern technology tends to alienate us from one another, increase daily stress levels, and leave many of us feeling dependent, inadequate, and incompetent. And many of us are terrified of the very technology on which we've become so dependent. For example, a 1993 national poll by Dell Computer Corporation of 1,000 adults and 1,000 teenagers found that 55% of the American population felt technophobic.

Consider, for example, Henry, who was a respected advertising manager responsible for a large staff. A corporate edict announced that he and all other managers in the company would receive a computer and would be expected to lead the transition to an automated office environment. Henry had done just fine using his typewriter for the last 20 years and saw no reason to switch now.

When the machine finally arrived and was installed, Henry didn't have the slightest idea what to do with it. With head pounding and palms sweating, he summoned his secretary, asked for an aspirin, and canceled his afternoon appointments. He said he felt as if he was coming down with the flu and decided to go home.

Of course, Henry didn't have the flu. In the face of a force he neither understood nor welcomed, Henry reacted with fright and flight. The anxiety, isolation, and sense of dread that Henry experienced is shared by many people when they must confront new technology.

It would be ridiculous to deny that technology has the capacity to enhance our lives. It would be equally silly to deny that it also can instill fear in the hearts of people who are normally cool-headed and quick to respond competently to traditional work, social, and family situations.

One might think that most people today would feel very comfortable with advanced technology. Microwaves heat our food. Computer programs check our work and instantly correct errors in spelling and math. Telephones, computers, faxes, and pagers provide 24-hour access to almost anybody anywhere. Desktop publishing enables us to create professional-looking documents faster and with more pizzazz than ever before. We can analyze, educate, organize, read, draw, listen to music, and even socialize without stepping away from the computer.

As wonderful as technology can be, however, it takes time and patience to acquire the knowledge and skills necessary to use these devices properly and at maximum efficiency. Many people are already short on time and patience because of the breakneck pace of the modern world. Add to that the human tendency to resist change, and the unfriendly nature of technology in general, and you end up with a recipe for frustration and failure.

As we saw in Henry's case, there is a dark side to the wonders of technology—and its called TechnoStress. In both subtle and not-so-subtle ways, people are paying a price for the pervasive and ever-expanding technological capabilities of the information age. Even as technology increases efficiency and expands human horizons, it is infringing on some of the most basic human needs.

Do you ever yearn to transact business with a bank teller, instead of an ATM, just for the personal contact? Does that make you feel hopelessly behind the times? Does your computer ever beep at you, indicating an invalid key sequence? Do you find yourself talking back to it in equally strident terms? Has your call waiting ever permitted a phone solicitor to interrupt an important conversation? The emotions that such experiences evoke—estrangement, embarrassment, and irritation—are signs of TechnoStress.

It is important to recognize that the seemingly tiny frustrations that people experience every day have a cumulative negative impact on psychological and physical health. Consider, for example, the TechnoStress that people experience every time they endure "technologically captive moments"—increments of time spent waiting for some machine-driven event to happen. Or when they silently question their actions because they have made decisions too quickly in response to an urgent fax, page, or e-mail. Think of how stressful it is to have to pretend to understand what the World Wide Web is during a business or social discussion. And what about assaults on one's senses by neon lights, digital displays, and computer-generated noises? Do they heighten technology-related anxiety? You bet they do.

As people endure these and similar experiences, the cumulative result is more than just a little frustration. Technology may do wonders **for** us, but it is also doing something **to** us. What it is doing is causing us TechnoStress.

The term technostress was coined in 1984 by Dr. Craig Brod, a clinical psychologist. He defined it as "a modern disease of adaptation caused by an inability to cope with the new computer technologies." We do not see TechnoStress as a disease however. We think of it as any negative impact on attitudes, thoughts, behaviors, or body physiology that is caused either directly or indirectly by technology.

Some TechnoStress does come directly from our experience with computers. But it is also caused by the overwhelming helplessness some people feel when trying to program a new VCR (videocassette recorder) or deal with a complicated voice mail system. Blood pressure rises, sleep is disrupted, and people slug down tablets for acid indigestion caused by stress.

Other types of TechnoStress are more subtle. People's attitudes and sense of safety are negatively affected when they feel that nothing they do is private anymore, or they worry that their jobs will become obsolete because of technology. These fears creep into their inner thoughts and undermine self-esteem. They are compounded if people believe they will never be able to learn how to use the new technology.

Technology even shapes human behavior. Some TechnoStressed adults ask their children to program the VCR. Others seek out time they can't really spare in order to transact business during banker's hours, rather than use ATMs. Avoidance of technology is one of the marks of a person who is TechnoStressed.

Technology is not going away. If anything, it will proliferate. But don't despair. There are ways to feel less frustrated and harried and to coexist peacefully with some of the world's awe-inspiring machines. This book provides strategies to help you maneuver your way through the technological maze. We'll show you how to recognize the difference between what you are able to do, thanks to technological advances, and what you are capable of handling as a person. You'll learn to preserve your humanity in our increasingly digital world by choosing the technology *you* want to use—and asserting control over it.

How Did We Come to This?

Imagine Rip van Winkle falling asleep in the early 1980s and awakening some 15 years later. How different the world would look! Even though we haven't slept through the past decade and a half, many of us are experiencing that same sense of shock and displacement. The world seems to have changed too rapidly. Wasn't it just a short time ago that computers were new and intriguing? When did everyone start talking about the World Wide Web?

Without a doubt, the present generation has seen more change in every aspect of life than any other. Consider this time line, which points out how quickly computer technology evolved after being introduced to the world:

10 B.C.	Abacus invented.
1440	Gutenberg invents printing from movable type.
1642	First mechanical adding machine invented.
1880	Automated weaving machine invented.
1946	First digital computer invented.
1969	First electronic link established between widely dispersed university computer networks—the Internet.
1975	Personal computer invented.
1982	First computer game, Pac-Man, is a hit.

7

| 1985–1990 | Computerized appliances and entertainment centers begin appearing in homes. |
| 1990 and beyond | Laptops, cellular phones, the World Wide Web, CD-ROMs, video-conferencing, and more electronic advancements appear. |

John Naisbitt predicted this technological turmoil in his 1982 book *Megatrends,* in which he noted that "change is occurring so rapidly that there is no time to react." More than a decade later, we are reacting by experiencing TechnoStress. In his prescription for our future, Naisbitt cautioned that to succeed, high tech must be counterbalanced by what he called "high touch"—the human response. He illustrated that when high touch is ignored when implementing technology, high tech encounters resistance.

Like Henry, humans tend to fight change. People thrive best in a predictable environment that is responsive to their needs and keeps life as uncomplicated as possible. Technology interferes with human nature on this very basic level. Have you ever gone to a store, for example, to replace a common household device, only to be deluged by such a wide assortment of new and improved models that you end up buying something that does more than you really wanted or needed? Or, have you found yourself in a situation where the item you want doesn't even come in an improved version—the manufacturer just stopped making it because it was too simple?

Our old, familiar, predictable world no longer exists and this frightens some people. Don't get us wrong. We like technology. We also like having choices; most people do. And that's what leads to a lot of their frustration with technology. In most cases, we have lost the choice to replace our favorite worn-out and broken machines with similar ones. We must always buy a new model. What if we liked our old one, which did exactly what we needed—and no more? Well, chances are it simply isn't manufactured any longer.

This frustration and disappointment is heightened by the constant bombardment of advertisements, news stories, and television shows that prod us to question everything we own. Is it fast enough? Does it do enough? Do I need a new one or should I upgrade the one I own? As soon as we buy a computer, we learn that a faster, better one will soon be available. No sooner do we sign up for a long-distance telephone service than we are told that another is more efficient and less expensive. It seems that we spend so much time questioning what we own that we have little time to enjoy it. This unsettled feeling contributes to technologically induced stress.

Uncertainty is also a factor. We never know where the next innovation will appear. Last year at a local movie theater, the familiar handles on the restroom sinks were changed to sensor controls. We watched people become perplexed and frustrated as they attempted the mundane task of washing their hands. A couple of months later, the gas pumps at the corner station were automated—gas couldn't be pumped until a credit card was swiped through the machine.

What's next? Every time new technology shows up, it has an effect on us. For some, new technology is fun. Most people, however, feel that it is anything but fun! In fact, the vast majority of us feel lost, inept, confused, frustrated, scared, angry, intimidated, and, most decidedly, unhappy. For instance, a 1995 Associated Press poll found that almost 50% of the over 1,000 American adults polled felt that the advance of technology is "leaving them behind."

Computerphobia to TechnoStress

To better understand this feeling of being left behind, let's take a short walk down memory lane and get a little historical perspective on today's TechnoStress.

Even before homes and offices had ever seen a desktop computer, public opinion was mixed, and a sense of foreboding was evident. In May 1963, Robert Lee, a social psychologist at IBM, conducted a nationwide study of 3,000 adults to "examine popular beliefs and attitudes about one of the prime symbols of our rapidly changing technology—the electronic computer." Lee found that the public held two independent beliefs:

Belief 1: Computers are useful tools of mankind.
Belief 2: Computers eventually will control society.

In the mid-1970s, as computer technology moved from laboratories into homes, social scientists continued to observe and measure public reaction. Surprisingly to some, research showed that many people had strong negative reactions to technology. They felt that computers were dehumanizing society, invading privacy, and taking away much-needed jobs.

By the early 1980s, computers were becoming more common, but they still struck fear into the hearts and minds of many people. Even as a small percentage of technophiles rushed to embrace the machines, a far greater number of individuals resisted the unfamiliar.

Claire, a professor at a small college near us, grew up loving computers. As a child, her parents took her to the University of California Computer Center open houses every year, where she was thrilled to watch a lab technician press a few buttons and make a picture of Mickey Mouse or some other popular character magically appear, ever so slowly, on a large sheet of paper.

As an adult, Claire remained excited about technology and was eager to apply it to her teaching. When a Radio Shack TRS-80 was brought onto her campus, she planned to use it to help psychology students learn statistics. She developed lesson plans and then walked into class the first day and excitedly announced to the 35 students that they were going to have the golden opportunity to learn statistics, not by hours of pushing buttons on calculators, but by letting a computer do the work in seconds.

Claire was shocked the next day when only 20 students showed up for class. Because this had never happened before, she tracked down the students who dropped the course and found that every one of them was afraid of actually learning to use a computer.

This fear of computers was quickly given a name— computerphobia. Timothy Jay first coined the term in 1981, but little was known about what caused it, who had it, and what could be done to overcome it. As psychologists and social scientists, we tackled the issue. Our studies of people and technology have now spanned more than 16 years and have involved more than 20,000 students, executives, office workers, teachers, children, parents, and community members in the United States and 22 other countries.

Our initial research focused on the use of personal computers in college courses. We studied anxiety levels, negative attitudes, and self-critical thoughts, and we discovered that about one-third of university students were computerphobic. And the problem wasn't just confined to students. In follow-up studies, we found that at least 25% and sometimes as many as half of the people in *any* group we studied qualified as computerphobic. And contrary to common stereotypes, the computerphobes were just as likely to be young as older and were equally divided between men and women.

To help these people, we developed the Computerphobia Reduction Program, which we ran during a three-year period in the late 1980s. Regardless of who the sufferer was (man or woman, child or adult), we found that computerphobia could be easily overcome. Utilizing cognitive-behavioral psychology principals in combination with our view of what was causing the problem, we worked with over 200 computerphobic university students, faculty, and staff, and we had a 92% success rate. Regardless of their original level of assessed computerphobia or technological discomfort (ranging from mild to severe), the participants became computer confident in *five hours or less!*

Our success did not come from teaching technology Instead, we taught computerphobes how to change the way they thought about technology or about themselves in relation to technology (stupid, dumb, inadequate, and so on) at school, at home, and elsewhere. In fact, they did not even touch any technology until their "graduation" from the program, for which they created their own computerized graduation certificate and proved their newfound comfort yet again. A six-month follow-up survey showed that our former computerphobes were purchasing and using the very technology they once feared and avoided.

Our knowledge base has continued to grow over the years. We have continued to see that negative attitudes and stresses related to technology can be changed. We have also developed clear guidelines as to how to best "learn" technology, which you'll read throughout the book. Many of the original ideas that helped our computerphobes become computer confident in the 1980s have led to the development of our tools used to combat today's TechnoStress.

As other products of technology became commonplace, the term "computerphobia" evolved into "technophobia." Today, both of these terms are used to describe a variety of negative reactions to technology. Although they may not have an actual fear of machines, we believe that almost everyone in modern society faces some kind of TechnoStress. Nationwide study after study support this conclusion:

▶ A 1994 MCI Communications study found that 49% of over 600 business executives surveyed nationwide were either cyberphobic or resistant to technology.

- A 1995 Equifax/Louis Harris poll found that almost 80% of consumers in the United States fear they've lost control of their computerized personal information.
- A 1995 Microsoft study of nearly 3,000 American adults found that 59% of respondents reported getting angry with their computers.
- A 1995 Times Mirror Center study of over 4,000 American adults found that 30% either dislike or have mixed feelings about computers and technology.
- A 1997 MCI One study of 1,000 adults found that 59% were hesitant, resistant, or frustrated about communication technologies.

Our own research continues to show that TechnoStress is running rampant in our society. Nearly every hour of the day brings people face-to-face with technology. And many of those encounters bring on TechnoStress.

Techno-Types: Which One Are You?

Not everybody reacts to technology in exactly the same way. Through our work we have found that people's reactions to new technology characteristically fall into three "Techno-Types": Eager Adopters, Hesitant "Prove Its," and Resisters. Just by their names you may have a good idea of which describes you best. Before we tell you more about these Techno-Types, take a guess at what percentage of Americans fall into each category.

GUESS THE TECHNO-TYPES

What percentage of Americans do *you* think fall into each of the following Techno-Types?

Percentage of Eager Adopters   ____

Percentage of Hesitant "Prove Its"   ____

Percentage of Resisters   ____

TOTAL   100%

Next, figure out your Techno-Type by taking the following quiz:

TECHNO-TYPE QUIZ

1. Suppose that for your birthday someone gives you a new electronic kitchen gadget (a coffeemaker or rice cooker, for example) that is completely computerized. Which of the following best describes how you would feel when you open the package and contemplate using this gadget?

   A. *Thrilled, excited, and eager. Can't wait to give it a try.*

   B. *Hesitant and wondering if you really need it. The way you do it now works just fine for you. Maybe you'll just put it away for now.*

   C. *Upset, worried, or nervous. Unsure of your ability to use it correctly. Considering how you can return it for something a bit more practical.*

   (continued)

15

TECHNO-TYPE QUIZ *(continued)*

2. When you want to record a television show that airs while you are at work, you:

    A. *Quickly, confidently, and easily program the VCR to record the show.*

    B. *Ask your son, daughter, or spouse to set the VCR, or find the manual and try to figure out how to do it. You know it's possible but are unsure that you'll be able to make it work.*

    C. *Squelch the thought, unless there is a handy person in the house to help. After all, aren't VCRs just for playing movies rented at Blockbuster?*

3. Your friend calls and tells you that he just bought a new state-of-the-art, souped-up multimedia computer system and wants you to come and see it. You:

    A. *Drop all your plans for the weekend, run right over on Saturday morning, and sit and play with the new toy for eight hours.*

    B. *Murmur words of congratulations and promise to get over to see it as soon as your schedule clears.*

    C. *Pretend to listen, adding appropriately placed "oh's" and "uh huh's," while clearly evading the request. (Not your idea of fun!)*

4. Now let's get back to that present you got in question 1—the new computerized gadget that does lots

of things. Now, picture yourself in the process of trying to learn to use it. Below is a list of 30 possible feelings. Check all the boxes that express your feelings in this situation.

☐ Amazed   ☐ Annoyed   ☐ Awkward

☐ Blocked   ☐ Calm   ☐ Composed

☐ Dumb   ☐ Eager   ☐ Excited

☐ Fantastic   ☐ Foolish   ☐ Frustrated

☐ Gratified   ☐ Great   ☐ Happy

☐ Helped   ☐ Hesitant   ☐ Intimidated

☐ Lost   ☐ Nervous   ☐ Overwhelmed

☐ Pleased   ☐ Relaxed   ☐ Relieved

☐ Self-conscious ☐ Successful   ☐ Triumphant

☐ Uncertain   ☐ Uncomfortable ☐ Upset

Scoring Instructions: For questions 1 through 3, if you answered (A) to two or more of the questions, you may be what we call an Eager Adopter. If you mostly answered (B), we would label you a Hesitant "Prove It," and if you answered mostly (C), you are a Resister. We'll score question 4 in a bit.

Now, let's learn more about these Techno-Types.

Eager Adopters

Eager Adopters love technology. Making up only 10 to 15% of the population, Eager Adopters are the first to buy new technological gadgets. The Eager Adopter views technology as fun and challenging. He or she (but it's usually a "he," as boys are more often socialized to be object-oriented, whereas girls are socialized to be people-focused) enjoys playing and tinkering. Technology holds a high, intrinsic attraction for Eager Adopters, who are literally drawn to it. When a problem arises—and technology does have its problems—the Eager Adopter either figures out the solution or finds someone who can.

Eager Adopters expect to have problems with technology. So, when a problem arises, they do not feel they have caused it. It is simply routine, and they are convinced that an answer is always close at hand. In fact, for the Eager Adopter, solving problems with technology can be fulfilling and satisfying. Our neighbor, Jerry, is the perfect example of an Eager Adopter. On trash day we see the boxes from Jerry's new purchases, and he spends the weekends tinkering with new gadgets. With his cellular phone to his ear, he talks to people about this setting or that switch while trying his new toys.

Hesitant "Prove Its"

Hesitant "Prove Its" account for between 50 and 60% of the population. They do not think technology is fun and prefer to wait until a new technology is proven before trying it. Even then, they hesitate to invest in the technology, wanting to be convinced they need something before buying it. But if you can show a Hesitant "Prove It" how something new will make life easier, he or she is willing to consider it.

The Hesitant "Prove It" knows there are problems with technology. Unlike an Eager Adopter, however, these people do not think solving such problems is fun. Hesitant "Prove Its" personalize any glitches and assume they created the problems. They also differ from Eager Adopters by not believing that solutions are readily available.

A relative of ours, Jo, is a perfect example of a Hesitant "Prove It." Although she is a very bright woman, she is unwilling to try a new technology unless someone comes and hooks it up and shows her the exact sequence of buttons to push. Then she carefully writes down the instructions and leaves them next to the machine. About six or seven years ago, Jo was given a VCR for Christmas. She looked at it and asked, "Why do I need one of these?" We hooked it up and showed her how to do some simple things, such as tape her favorite soap opera. She loved it and now uses it almost every day to tape her "show"—but she never tapes anything else but that one show. And when something goes wrong with the VCR, she calls one of us to fix it, because she is afraid to experiment with buttons she doesn't understand. Although she's now a VCR fan, she's still a Hesitant "Prove It."

Resisters

Resisters *avoid* technology. The second-largest Techno-Type, at 30 to 40% of the population, Resisters want nothing to do with technology, no matter what anyone says or does to convince them that some of it is useful. Technology is absolutely no fun for these people, who are certain that they will break any machine or gadget that they touch. Because of this, they feel intimidated, embarrassed, or downright stupid. And, sadly, because they generally believe they are the only ones who feel this way, they do not talk about it; they simply try to avoid the technology. Henry, whom we introduced at the beginning of this chapter, is a Resister.

As Henry discovered, technology cannot be avoided forever. Hence, when forced to use technology, Resisters do so slowly and with difficulty. When a technological problem arises, Resisters are certain it is their fault. Problems with technology are severe blows to a Resister's self-esteem and confidence—and each new problem makes the Resister run further away from technology. Frank, a highly resistant psychologist in one of our studies, owns a computer, but because he cannot get it to work and feels too embarrassed to ask for help, he covered it with a cloth and turned it into a plant stand.

Check Your Feelings

Do you recognize yourself in any of these types so far? Let's move on to question 4 from the Techno-Type Quiz. Half the feelings listed are positive and half are negative. Did you check more positive or more negative feelings? Let's see how you compare to others. In an in-depth study, we asked people how they would react under similar circumstances. The following table lists the feelings checked by at least one-third of each group, with the *most common reactions* from the top down.

Eager Adopters	Hesitant "Prove Its"	Resisters
Excited	Uncomfortable	Frustrated
Amazed	Uncertain	Nervous
Eager	Awkward	Awkward
Great	Eager	Uncertain
Successful	Excited	Amazed
Relaxed	Amazed	Dumb
Frustrated	Dumb	Overwhelmed
Pleased	Hesitant	Upset
	Upset	Uncomfortable
	Annoyed	Hesitant
	Frustrated	
	Self-conscious	

Notice that Eager Adopters expressed mostly positive feelings, but they would feel frustrated, too. Frustration is part of the technology experience, even for people who enjoy it. The Hesitant "Prove Its" selected feelings that highlight their ambivalence. On one hand they certainly feel uncomfortable, uncertain, and awkward, but as seen lower on the list, they can also be eager and excited. And, finally, Resisters nearly unilaterally said they feel frustrated, nervous, and plain miserable.

How did your feelings compare? Some of you may have different reactions to different types of technologies. Toward technology that is more familiar or already mastered, you may feel like an Eager Adopter. But when a new machine or gadget comes your way, you may be hesitant or even resistant.

Now, back to how the rest of the population scored:

10 to 15% are Eager Adopters.
50 to 60% are Hesitant "Prove Its."
30 to 40% are Resisters.

These numbers may surprise you, but our experience has shown that people generally overestimate the technological comfort of others. They usually believe they are the only ones who are resistant to or intimidated by technology. This is important to recognize because it is the more typical reaction to feel ill at ease with and TechnoStressed by technology than otherwise. From all the research we've read and conducted, we estimate that 85 to 90% of the population is not eagerly embracing technology. Because technology is being thrust upon them at a pace and volume greater than they desire, this vast majority of the populace is also experiencing TechnoStress.

No Way to Escape

Now that computers seem to be built into everything from thermometers to televisions and automobiles, TechnoStress really hits us on all levels; there is no way to escape from it. From that pesky digital alarm clock (which never goes off at the right time because it is unnecessarily complicated to set) through our VCR (which never seems to tape the right show), we are assaulted by complex contraptions. As Donald Norman, an engineer-turned-psychologist, so aptly wrote in his book, *The Design of Everyday Things:*

Why do we put up with the frustrations of everyday objects, with objects that we can't figure out how to use . . . with washing machines and dryers that have become too confusing to use, with audio-stereo-television-video-cassette-recorders that claim in their advertisements to do everything, but that make it almost impossible to do anything? . . . Poorly designed objects can be difficult and frustrating to use. They provide no clues—or sometimes false clues. They trap the user and thwart the normal process of interpretation and understanding. . . . The result is a world filled with frustration.

What is TechnoStress Doing to Us?

All of this adds up to a growing revolt against technology. This antitechnology backlash is fueled by books such as Clifford Stoll's *Silicon Snake Oil* and Stephen Talbott's *The Future Does Not Compute,* which depict a world in which people are besieged by machines. There is even a national organization devoted to resisting technology, called the Lead Pencil Club. They proudly proclaim in their manifesto, "We will avoid fax and hang up on voice mail. We will receive no e-mail and send none. If our computers develop a virus, we will seek no cure. Our communications will be face to face. If direct human contact is not possible, we will write letters in our own handwriting because that handwriting is a mark of our personality." And, according to media reports, membership in the Lead Pencil Club is growing at a staggering pace.

Another, even larger, anti-technology groundswell emanates from a group calling itself the Neo-Luddites. Taking their name and cue from a group of nineteenth-century textile workers who fought to stop the industrialization of England's clothing industry, Neo-Luddites are battling twentieth-century technology. Neo-Luddites firmly believe the world was better before sliced bread, and their movement seems to be gaining momentum.

We can understand the feelings that Neo-Luddites and Lead Pencil Club members have toward technology. We can certainly understand why they would want us all to JUST SAY NO to technology. But we do not believe this is the answer. We believe that each of us needs to find our own personal balance.

Change is a natural part of our existence. We have continued to evolve and change to the betterment of our species. This is part of what it means to be human. And now, technology presents us with nearly infinite opportunities for greater change. To blindly accept all technology is certainly a mistake. Often, there may be greater benefit doing something the "old-fashioned way." But to eschew all technology as evil, without evaluating its contribution to our lives, is not the answer.

We believe that the answer lies in evaluating each form of technology on its own merits, then weighing its benefits. We must then learn to use the technologies we choose, without experiencing TechnoStress. And we need to learn to experience this technological era in a way that allows us to come to terms with it, without feeling intruded upon or personally undermined. Only by doing this will we be able to change, grow, and prosper in our current world.

The Time Is Right for Overcoming TechnoStress

This book is intended to shed light on the complex, emotional and experiential impact our high-tech world is having on us and our day-to-day reality. Empowered by knowledge, we can make choices. The ability to make educated choices creates a sense of being in control of one's life.

In the following chapters, we explore how technology works both for and against us, illustrate how different people experience its impact, and offer guidelines for setting clear and consistent human boundaries in this technological era. In chapters devoted to each of the arenas in which technology affects us—at work, at home, and at play—we expose the invisible or only vaguely apparent stresses that wear away at one's sense of efficacy. Our goals are to illuminate what makes us susceptible to TechnoStress and to show how to take control over the machines in our lives.

By allowing technological advances into our lives, we hope to enrich ourselves. But there is a delicate balance between technological efficiency and TechnoStress. To get the most from technology we must choose between what *we actually need and want,* what *we think we need and want,* and *what we are told we need and should want.* In the shadow of amazing technological advances, we can easily forget that it is our capacity to dream, to intuit, to compromise, to negotiate, and to create with spontaneity and vision that gave birth to the very technology with which we are now struggling to keep pace. If we are going to preserve our humanity—and sanity—in an increasingly technologized world, it is these qualities that we must seek to preserve.

2

The Myth of Technological Ease

‹ ‹ ‹ ‹ ‹ ‹ ‹ › › › › › › ›

I magine spending a pleasant evening at home, watching a favorite television show. A commercial comes on for the newest state-of-the-art computer. "It's simple," the spokesperson says, "You just open the box, plug in a few cords, and in minutes you can create beautiful three-fold brochures, balance your checkbook, or produce personalized birthday cards."

If the media hype is true, if computers are really easier than ever to use, why do the majority of those learning to use them find it an incredibly difficult and frustrating task? And:

- ► Why have technical support calls increased at most major computer companies more than 50% over the last several years—to well over 100,000 per month?
- ► If everything is supposed to be as simple as "plug and play," why did a 1996 *Orlando Sentinel* article report that 1 in 10 purchased computers are returned?
- ► If computers and technology have become so "user friendly," why have survey after survey found that people are becoming increasingly frustrated with their computers?

People and technology are like oil and water: They do not mix easily. No one can just sit down in front of a computer for the first time and learn the machine. Most people will pick up the mouse and point it at the screen like a Star Trek phaser. That is because technology does not experience, act, or think as we do. There is no inherent fit between people and machines. People do not process information in the same way computers do.

Much is known about how people's brains operate. Current thinking suggests that the human brain can be viewed as containing three major parts—sensory memory, short-term memory, and long-term memory—all working at the same time and in conjunction with each other. Let's illustrate how these three systems work by looking at what happens as you meet a friend on the street and have a short conversation about the weather.

As you are walking down the street, your brain is bombarded by information from all your sensory organs. Your eyes see trees, concrete, buildings, people, and much more, all seemingly in a series of glances. Your ears hear the traffic, dogs barking, people talking, music from a boom box, and even the whir of rollerblades approaching from behind. Your nose gets a whiff of a tantalizing perfume followed immediately by cooking hot dogs and car exhaust. Your body registers the light breeze on your face and the warmth of the sun on your back.

All of these sensations and more are perceived by your body at the same time. It would be overwhelming for you to attend to all of them, so the brain must be selective. Your sensory memory's job is to sort them out and determine which to attend to and which to ignore. Fortunately for your sanity, sensory memory, while able to attend to many sensations, only retains each for a few seconds. Sensory memory's lifework is to grab selected sensations and pass them on to the short-term memory to be interpreted and understood.

Short-term memory, also called working memory, tries to make sense of the sensations that it receives by using what it already knows in long-term memory. In essence, short-term memory acts as a mental way station. As information enters from sensory memory, short-term memory, with help from long-term memory, decides which is important enough to be stored in long-term memory and which it will discard completely. So, as you see your friend, your sensory memory passes his picture on to short-term memory, which accesses information from long-term memory to remind yourself all about him.

In contrast to sensory memory, short-term memory has a limited capacity, which has been estimated to be between five and nine "chunks" of information. This was demonstrated in a famous experiment entitled "The Magical Number Seven, Plus or Minus Two," by George Miller. A chunk can be a single number or word or perhaps a group of numbers or words that go together. Short-term memory's limited capacity explains why we can nearly always remember a telephone number that is told to us, without writing it down, but why we have a more difficult time remember longer strings of numbers like those found on our credit cards. If we want to memorize our 16-digit Visa card number (say, 0673088931201946) we might try breaking it into eight chunks: 06–73–08–89–31–20–19–46. Now we are in the realm of our short-term memory's storage capabilities.

Short-term memory is only capable of holding information for a brief period—up to 20 seconds or so—unless it is repeated over and over. So, if the operator tells you a phone number and you dial it immediately, you will probably have no trouble remembering all the digits. However, if the number is busy and you have to dial it again later, the only way to keep it in short-term memory is to repeat it over and over again to yourself. Since short-term memory also brings in information stored in your long-term memory in order to help you understand and interpret newly arriving sensations, and since short-term memory is very small, the new information pushes out the old information, which is gone forever.

Information in short-term memory is constantly transferred into long-term memory through rehearsal and embellishment. So, when your friend tells you about his new job, you are able to transfer that information into the long-term memories that you already have about him.

Long-term memory is capable of holding vast amounts of information for a long time. Unfortunately, for humans, retrieving that information is not always so easy. This is why we can recognize the face of someone we haven't seen or thought about for many years, but we can't always recall their name or how we know them.

Now, let's briefly look at how a computer works. Similar to our sensory memory, a computer gets its information from an external source. Either through the keyboard, a disk, a modem, or some other piece of equipment, information is brought into the computer. Like a human being, the computer has a working memory, called RAM—short for random access memory. And like our short-term memory, RAM is limited in its space. Finally, similar to our long-term memory, a computer has a hard disk where vast amounts of information can be saved for long periods of time.

With all these similarities in structure, it is tempting to assert that humans and computers process information in the same ways. But this is simply not true. Where our human sensory memory is quite transitory, a computer can gobble up as much information as fast as you can feed it. Want to increase the speed at which a computer "thinks"? Just get a faster processor. Not so with our brains. While our short-term memory is limited to five to nine chunks, add more RAM and the computer's working memory is increased. And, barring hard disk crashes, computers never forget anything or have difficulty retrieving information.

Even though we seem to have the same processing pieces, the way we use them is quite different. Humans can think a multitude of thoughts and perform many actions simultaneously, while computers can only perform actions one step at a time. Humans can be intuitive, emotional, creative, and inventive, while computers only follow programmed instructions. Humans are sensitive to nonverbal cues—a raised eyebrow, a sad expression—while computers are not. The result is certain friction when these two mismatched operating styles are brought together.

Why Is Technology So Alien?

So, we know that people think differently than machines. In addition, we need to realize that technology is not necessarily smart. Donald Norman has written a series of books (*The Design of Everyday Things, Things That Make Us Smart,* and *Turn Signals Are the Facial Expressions of Automobiles*) discussing why technology is difficult for most of us to use. Using a wide range of examples, Norman suggests that what the designer has in mind when creating the device is not the same as what the user understands when he or she tries to use it. While the designer strives for *function*—what and how much can it do?—the user craves *form*—how can I use it? Norman tells us about knobs that seem like they should turn but instead need to be pushed. He describes how people unsuccessfully attempt to find the right sequence of buttons to push to set digital clocks or to program VCRs. Because the sequence of steps is not inherently sensible, people don't remember how to do it without the manual. Yet when people can't get some new gadget to work right, they assume *they* have a problem. But often, it is not the person—it's the machine. The design of the equipment and the functions are often so convoluted that nobody could get them to work, even with the manual.

Why are machines so complicated? One reason is that today's technology is invisible. When many of us were growing up, most broken things could be taken apart, fixed, and put back together. We saw our television with the back off and could see the tube being replaced. If the vacuum cleaner stopped suctioning, the bottom could be removed, the belt replaced, and it could be put back together. Mechanical things were fixable.

Computerized technology changed that. Tearing apart a computer, one finds boards and miniaturized computer chips whose functions don't relate to their form. No longer are there understandable pieces, such as tubes, pulleys, belts, or gears, that allow us to make some sense of how these machines run.

And how do they work anyway? How does e-mail really traverse vast distances? What happens inside a fax machine? Technology's workings are not obvious. We have difficulty understanding what we can't see, touch or fix. And it is human nature to fear or avoid what we can't understand or explain.

If it is hard to see today's technology, it is equally difficult to hear it. The language of technology is not of this world. RAM. ROM. Bits. Bytes. Baud rates. Megahertz. The Internet. The World Wide Web. Intimidating foreign jargon abounds. In a study of 542 business people conducted in late 1995, we asked if participants understood the terms "on-line service," "Internet," and "Information Super-highway." Nearly half said they knew very little or nothing about these buzzwords. Yet this jargon peppers newspaper reports and magazine articles. These new terms, phrases, and technospeak do nothing but create alienation—dividing people into two very separate groups that we call the "Knows" and the "Know-Nots." Most of us are "Know-Nots."

Not only is technospeak foreign, it's also vague. The meaning of the words is not self-evident. The word "freezer" describes its function: It freezes things. A dishwasher washes dishes. These terms are useful and leave no room for confusion or misunderstanding. But in the new parlance, what does "hard drive" mean? How about "modem"? These words don't invoke mental images or trigger links to our existing knowledge base. People learn by assimilating new information into their existing rubrics of understanding—called mental schemata. But without visual or verbal cues, it is impossible to figure out which schema should come into play. The language and the form give no clues for relational learning.

Technology is hard to understand, yet it seems to be everywhere. Every magazine ad and television commercial carries an Internet address these days. And there is a great deal of media attention on "surfing the Web." Because of the ubiquitous focus on technology, everyone assumes that they are the only ones not riding the wave. For example, in a study of 326 adults conducted just a year ago, we found that respondents **overestimated** the number of people who were on-line by a factor of three! In fact, according to a 1997 report by Forrester Research, only 15%

of the population even has access to e-mail. Research by Intelliquest, Dataquest, International Data Corporation, and other survey companies shows that less than 15% have ever visited the World Wide Web. Even though the "Knows" represent less than 20% of the population, "Know-Nots" erroneously feel that it is they who are in the minority, not the majority.

What Makes Technology So Hard to Learn?

Why does approximately eighty-five percent of the population fall into the "Know Not" category? Poor design, invisible mechanisms, and nonsuggestive language combine to make technology intimidating. These issues are exacerbated by the fact that most people don't receive the kind of instruction they need when learning new technology.

Turning to a book or instruction manual on how to operate a new machine will likely end in frustration. Most manuals have not been written with sound educational principles in mind. The grammar is poor, sentences often make no sense, and instructions are unclear and peppered with jargon. Guidelines often omit crucial steps that are obvious to the writer (an Eager Adopter, no doubt) but are not obvious to the reader. Educational research demonstrates the importance of good visuals. Yet technical manuals consist primarily of words, with few pictures.

If stymied by the books, there are always courses. But that path, too, is fraught with perils. A few years back, we performed a study of technophobia at an aerospace company. Employees took a voluntary, three-day workshop on the computer topic of their choice. The study showed that 30% of the employees were more technophobic after the workshop than they had been before. Why? No matter how interesting the topic, people can't concentrate on new information eight hours a day. After an hour or so, the brain shuts down and assimilating any new material is next to impossible. Even technology classes that meet for only a short time pose problems, since the teacher is usually a very excited Eager Adopter. It is easy for them to use the computer, so these instructors speak rapidly, use excessive jargon, and assume the students are all keeping up.

Another problem with classes is that the level of the learners usually varies greatly within the group. The Eager Adopters will get bored if the instructor teaches to the Hesitant "Prove Its" and Resisters' needs. The Hesitant "Prove Its" and Resisters will become lost and intimidated if the instructor teaches at a level appropriate for Eager Adopters. And if the teacher aims for somewhere in between, everyone ends up frustrated.

When books and courses fail, most people turn to friends and colleagues. More than likely, however, the only people you know who could answer your questions are Eager Adopters. They will probably talk fast, throw around jargon, and don't realize that they might be confusing you. Or they may simply take over and do it for you, leaving you without the experience of learning how to solve your own problems and feeling pretty inadequate.

Although the myth of technological ease has been dispelled, technology itself isn't going anywhere. So how can technology be made to work for people? The first trick is to learn how to learn about technology. We need to be able to learn, become confident, and experience mastery over technology.

How Do We Learn?

So how do people learn? It depends. Joan, for example, was a bright, efficient office manager. She had mastered a complex new filing system in a day. But she couldn't keep up with the computer class she was taking at a local college. She liked the teacher but couldn't follow his rapid-fire presentation of material. Yet, when she read the textbook, she caught on quickly. Joan was a good self-teacher, but not a great lecture hall student. Some people process verbal information quickly. Others need visual stimulation. Some students need coaching or tutoring. Others do better when they learn at their own pace. The key to learning is knowing your own preferences and strengths.

Beginning as a child, each person develops, tests, and refines a unique system for taking in new information. Educators refer to this system as a "learning style." It encompasses how a person takes in, stores, and retrieves information. Learning style is composed of preferences from environmental, emotional, social, and physical elements. Interestingly, the learning styles of husbands and wives, and of parents and children, tend to differ dramatically.

The learning styles of siblings also tend to be more different from each other than similar.

These differences in learning style can pose some hefty hurdles when it comes to learning technology. For example, if your spouse shows you how to set the VCR, he or she is teaching you from their method of understanding. This may not work for you. In fact, your styles may be so different that the way your spouse is trying to explain the process may make no sense. The secret to mastering new technology is to identify the components of your individual learning style and then tailor the mode of instruction to your needs. This means discovering the elements of your learning style.

Environmental Elements

Each of us has a preferred atmosphere for learning. Researchers have found that sound, lighting, temperature, furniture, and surroundings can have a significant impact on a person's ability to focus and learn. Think about where you used to study when you had final examinations in high school. Did you need absolute quiet or did soft music help you concentrate? Or were you one of those people who actually studied better with rock music blaring in your room? Where did you plunk yourself down to study? Outside or inside? In bright or soft light? Bundled up and warm or in shorts even when it was chilly outside? Whatever your choices, you picked them because they worked for you. And these choices are not set in stone. Your environmental preferences can and will change as you change.

Emotional Elements

How people feel about what they are learning and how they approach the task of learning also affects success. There are three important emotional dimensions to one's learning style: motivation, persistence, and internal versus external structure.

Motivation

Motivated learners are raring to go. They need only be told what to do and how to get help if needed. Unmotivated learners are another story. Simply telling them to learn something will never suffice. They may procrastinate or start the process and then get sidetracked and never finish. Unmotivated learners need to be given short learning tasks, a rationale as to the importance of each task, and a lot of positive reinforcement for their accomplishments. The process of completing small tasks on the road to the goal helps unmotivated learners build internal motivation and take pride in their accomplishments.

Persistence

Persistent learners work at a task until it is completed. Those without this stick-to-itiveness will be forgetful and disorganized, lose interest, and become irritated. Varying the length and type of the task, permitting breaks, allowing them to switch from task to task, and giving clear expectations of what is to be accomplished within a certain time frame will help keep, people who lack persistence on track.

Internal versus External Structure

People need structure. For some, the structure is generated internally. Others need external forces to impose structure. Those who operate from an internal structure can map out their own game plan as to how best approach a task. They like to do things their own way, and their way works for them. Those in need of external structure prefer having someone else tell them exactly what to do. They are happiest when they have a clear working plan in which someone has laid out all of the steps. Both internally and externally driven people can learn; they just need to be taught differently. Internally controlled learners often like to set up their own learning environment rather than learn in someone else's. Give an internal person a general idea of what needs to be learned and then turn them loose. Externally driven people need a bit more structure—such as having a teacher break a task into workable parts, make suggestions, give clear directions, and provide assistance when needed.

Social Elements

Do you like to learn alone, with one other person, or in a group? Each of these styles works, but you have to recognize your preferences if you want to learn technology successfully. Do you work better when you have an authoritative instructor (one you are sure can answer any and all of your questions), or do you prefer learning from a colleague or friend who may not know all the answers? You can do it either way, but it is best if it is your choice.

Physical Elements

People learn with their brain, but the brain is part of the body, and body states influence learning. The body's rhythm of daily high and low energy fluctuations affects the learning style. Some people cannot function well at the same time of day that others are at their best. Think about when you feel the freshest and most ready to take in new information. When is your concentration at its worst? Using this information and coordinating your learning schedule with your best time of day makes for success. If you try to learn something new when your body is telling you that it wants to take a nap, your prospects are dim.

Information enters the brain through three main channels: sound (our auditory channel), sight (our visual channel), and touch or body movement (our tactile and kinesthetic channels). Educators are well aware that we each have a preferred learning channel. People introduced to new material through their preferred channel remember significantly more. Auditory learners must hear what they are learning to really understand it. Visual learners learn by seeing. These people do well using videotape or film, interactive computer software, and by reading. Tactile-kinesthetic learners need to feel and touch in order to learn. They need to have real-life experiences in order to better absorb and retain.

Children need to learn how to learn. Along with this, most of what they learn is brand new. So, in essence, while they are learning they are building a conceptual framework for understanding and organizing their world of new information. Children learn best initially through a combination of tactile-kinesthetic and visual channels. Auditory information can be used as a backup, but it is through the hands-on play time along with repetition, repetition, repetition that they best incorporate new information. Watch young children and you will see them thrill over playing with the same doll for 45 consecutive days. It is this combination of repetition and active hands-on manipulation that helps them learn.

As people move through their developmental stages, they become better able to take in additional information through auditory channels alone. By high school and certainly by college, lecture is the main way that teachers transmit information. Using the framework developed during the elementary years, people assimilate additional information into categories or subjects already existing in their memory. However, when people are faced with new learning situations that run counter to anything they have experienced before, the best learning tactic is to go back to square one and reembrace the combination of tactile-kinesthetic and visual channels that worked so well for them when they were children. People need to touch, feel, and practice, practice, practice in order to build the new structures and framework. This is exactly what humans need when developing the framework that will incorporate information about technology.

What Is Your Optimal Learning Environment?

Close your eyes and think about the way you learn best today. Picture your optimal learning environment, considering these factors:

- Time of day (morning, early afternoon, evening, nighttime?).
- Noise level (soft music, rock and roll, quiet?).
- Lighting (bright, dim, natural daylight, fluorescent, halogen?).
- People (alone or around others?).
- Temperature (slightly cool or warm?).
- Learning preferences (alone by reading, touching, seeing, practicing, or being taught by someone one-on-one or in a group?).

Now that you've identified your optimal learning environment, it's time to figure out *what* you want to learn.

Stimulating the Learning Process

High motivation is essential for success. What you learn should have a high personal value to you—a hook to draw you into the process—in order to build your motivation to learn and use the technology. So, at first pick something that is VERY practical, and you REALLY want to know. For example, one of the best ways to teach someone word processing is by first showing them how to write a letter to a friend or family member.

When we teach the World Wide Web, we ask the learners about their hobbies or special interests and then show them how to find that information immediately. For one student it was finding Italian risotto recipes. For an amateur archeologist, visiting Aztec ruins electronically was a thrill. A busy executive might be motivated by learning

43

how to use the distribution list in her voice mail system so she can send the same message to her whole staff at once. Everyone's hook is different. Once you find yours, learning new technology will become much more exciting.

When you've found your hook, limit your learning sessions to an hour or so. Learning sessions that last for hours may work for other content areas, but they don't work when learning technology. Intensive training sessions overload cognitive capacity and increase anxiety levels. Instead, technology needs to be learned with plenty of breaks, to allow time for the new material to be assimilated.

Remember what we said about tactile learning? Get your hands on the equipment early and often. The sooner you get your hands on the machine and press the buttons or keys or move that mouse, the faster you will learn. Even if you have no earthly idea of what you are doing, you need to be in direct physical contact with the technology. As you gain experience with the machine, you'll also gain a sense of success and mastery, which builds your confidence and helps keep you motivated.

As we have seen, technology and people are like oil and water, so as you learn, there will be times when you feel frustrated, inadequate, and alienated. Keep at it anyway. Whenever people learn something new, they make mistakes and feel awkward. Don't let that dampen your determination. It takes practice to master a new skill.

Perhaps the biggest mistake we see is when a learner struggles with a manual and tries to go it alone. There is only a small chance that a person can successfully learn technology from a manual. Oh, sure, manuals do serve a useful function. When you get stuck and have a specific question, a good manual (with a large index or detailed table of contents) can be a great help. So, here's what we recommend: Find yourself a "personal trainer."

This is not someone who will push you to do just five more leg lifts. Your personal technology trainer needs to be knowledgeable, yet calm and relaxed, and should know something about you, your level of knowledge, and how to explain what you want to learn. Your trainer should be able to talk about technology clearly, without resorting to jargon, and should break down the process into workable steps, explaining the rationale for each. A trainer's style should not be evaluative or arrogant, but should be patient and encouraging (never making little quips such as, "See how easy this is" or "This is a piece of cake").

You have some responsibility here, too. You need to feel comfortable about taking control of the training time. You must stop your trainer if there is something you do not understand and you should ask to have it explained again, perhaps in a different way. Your trainer should demonstrate a few steps at a time and then let you try them. You need to develop confidence, and it will only happen with you in the driver's seat!

BEWARE! Most trainers are Eager Adopters. And most Eager Adopters just can't resist showing you how to do something by reaching over and pressing the keys for you. This does you little good. Watching an Eager Adopter rapidly press a series of keys gets the task done, but it may diminish your self-confidence. You need to press the keys. If your personal trainer does it for you rather than walking you through the process make sure to say, "Tell me how to do it and let me press the keys."

Imitate the Masters

Technology has problems and problems are normal. Sometimes the user pushes a wrong button. Other times the problem lies with a developer, who produced a confusing manual, or the manufacturer, who did not assemble the machine correctly. Whatever the cause, mishaps are inevitable. So take a lesson from the Eager Adopters. They expect problems and see them as puzzles to solve. They believe an answer will be available and find it a challenge to master. Learn to expect problems and soon those problems will not feel like personal assaults.

People who are successful at mastering technology use two strategies when faced with a glitch: They seek help from another person, or they attempt to solve the problem on their own. Either way, they keep at it until they find a solution. Those who are not successful with technology use a strategy of avoidance. When confronted by a technological problem, they walk away. Remember, up to 85% of the population has some degree of discomfort with technology. You are not alone when you feel confused or frustrated. If you feel it, others must as well, so be a problem solver or get help. People like the image of having some support person on a "technological" tether. Just a quick tug, and they are there.

When problems arise, the longer people sit with the frustration, the more they will come to dislike the technology or feel inadequate. You need support when the inevitable problem occurs that you can't solve easily. Have your personal trainer agree to be available by phone to help you out and to return your calls as soon as possible, to reduce your frustration and increase your confidence. Know where your computer-savvy friends are when you start practicing and reach out as needed.

Learning is much more effective if people learn on the same equipment that they are going to eventually use. The more similar the equipment, the easier and faster the knowledge can be transferred. This is why, for example, it is easier for children to learn to tie shoes by wearing the same shoes over a period of time rather than learning to tie a variety of different lace styles at the same time. The lesson to be learned is to have your personal trainer come to you and teach you on your computer. Or make sure the class uses the same equipment and software you plan to use at home or work.

Just as children use repetition to internalize new information, the best way to learn to use any technology is to give yourself ample time to experiment and play. Playtime needs to be nonpressured and not under the watchful eye of a supervisor. In essence, you have to allow yourself to become a child again, willing and eager to experiment, play, and explore the world. And the frustration you experience when learning new technology will begin to dissipate.

You Don't Have to Learn It All or Have It All

You will further widen your comfort zone if you recognize that there is more technology out there than you will ever be able to learn or use. There are also more magazines published than any one person can keep up with. With technology, like magazines, you get to select what you want and only use what works for you. Don't worry about the rest; you are in charge of making the choices.

3

Where Are the Boundaries in a Virtual World?

‹   ‹   ‹   ‹   ‹   ‹   ‹   ›   ›   ›   ›   ›   ›   ›

The ability to be in charge of technology has had a bearing on the human condition ever since we started creating gadgets to help us accomplish day-to-day tasks. Having that sense of mastery over machines is even more critical today, when it is so easy to feel that technology has taken control of our lives.

Not so long ago, people worked from nine to five. When they left the office, they were done working and knew it with certainty. If they went to a movie for an

evening of peaceful, uninterrupted pleasure, the only possible concern was whether to have a medium or large
buttered popcorn. At home, telephone calls came from
friends or relatives.

Today, all that has changed. We go to see a show and
our concentration is interrupted three times by pagers going off. We check our voice mail or e-mail from home in
the evening and often feel a need to respond before the
next workday. During dinner time, we are interrupted by
computer-driven cold callers who may not even be in our
time zone. Cars have become mobile telephone booths,
and even vacation packing now includes a laptop and sky
pager, because the idea of going just one day without
"connecting" is disquieting.

Technology is invading our boundaries from all sides.
Not only are people feeling physically, auditorally, and visually violated, they are also doing the same thing to others, perhaps without even realizing it. The proliferation of
communication technology over the last few years has
given us a multitude of ways to find and connect with others. However, we are doing so with something akin to impulsive abandon, not thinking before calling a friend's car
phone or considering whether it is a true emergency before paging someone. Because we can get to them, we do.

Even though many people fear and resent technology,
through conditioning they have become dependent upon
it. For example, we get irritated if we call someone and
they don't have an answering machine or voice mail system. We call home from work and elsewhere to retrieve

messages from our own machines. We leave our pagers on 24 hours a day and expect others to do the same.

This growing dependence affects us negatively. We count on our technology to research, spruce up, and spell check important work. We rely on it to videotape our favorite television shows and to reheat leftovers quickly. Then we slip into a crisis when the computer crashes, the microwave dies, or the phone lines go down on our Internet server. People allow themselves to be sucked into this technological abyss, and in doing so they become more machine-oriented and less sensitive to their own needs and the needs of others. Some people become so immersed in technology that they risk losing their identities. When is enough enough? Where are the boundaries?

Human Boundary Needs

Infants have no sense of "I." Their identity is merged with that of their primary caretakers. They share a state of oneness with their parents, which makes them feel safe and whole. They get instant attention by uttering a cry. In babies, self-absorption and the desire for instant gratification are acceptable and even expected.

As they develop physically, infants become more and more aware of their separateness. First they crawl. Later they can walk away. Yet, even with this growing independence, toddlers need boundaries to feel safe and calm.

Although they are mobile and starting to explore the world by themselves, they are too young and inexperienced to know how to create safe boundaries. Parents have the job of defining the boundaries and setting limits. However, even when limits are set, a child's nature is to test and push up against them.

If there are clear limits, and a child repeatedly bumps into them, his behavior stays relatively under control. By virtue of the consistency, he feels calm, safe, and secure. He knows what he can and cannot do. However, when no limits are present, or if they are unclear, inconsistent, or suddenly disappear, the child becomes distressed and begins to act out and feel out of control. This behavior signals that boundaries need to be reestablished.

As the mind develops, children first babble, then talk, and eventually form opinions different from their parents. Their sense of "I," or self, emerges. Each person's sense of self evolves into very clear emotional and physical boundaries. They learn who they are and who they are not, what they can and cannot do. They establish, literally and figuratively, where they start and stop. By the time they reach adulthood, most people are aware of the personal boundaries that help them feel whole, complete, and safe.

As they mature, children develop patience and learn to tolerate delay. This becomes an important aspect of an adult's ability to think things through, rather than act impulsively. However, at their core stays the ever-eager child who wants things NOW, who wants to have his needs instantly met, who can be very self-absorbed. By keeping a watchful eye on the balance between impulse and thought-out action, people are able to balance their needs with the needs of others and the realities of life.

Then along comes technology, and people are thrust into the "terrible twos" again. They are like young children who are out of control. This is because technology has dislodged boundaries and changed the rules. So, people push to see if and where new limits exist. What they are discovering is that the limits far exceed what we ever deemed possible. Technology excites our impulsive side by allowing us to do fantastic things, even if they are not in our best interest. Like children, we must learn once again to observe boundaries.

A key step toward achieving technological maturity is reestablishing boundaries, beginning with the borders that protect our perceived and actual personal space. Humans tend to do this instinctively.

Try this experiment. Walk up to a friend, stand a comfortable distance away, and begin a conversation. Now, slowly move closer to your friend, while you continue speaking. In all likelihood, as you move closer, your friend will begin to move backward in an attempt to maintain distance between you. We all have optimal interpersonal space of about three feet. This space provides a comfort zone for us and we strive to maintain it.

Our other space need is for perceptual space. Perceptual space, which spans much more than three feet, is the area in which we are aware of sights, sounds, and smells without necessarily being conscious of them. People are alert to changes in this area and strive to maintain its sanctity. Perceptual space can be invaded, too. Sudden movements caught by the corner of the eye that cause you to turn your head, or unexpected odors that grab your attention are invasions of perceptual space.

People's strong need to maintain control over their interpersonal and perceptual space comes from our inborn need for self-preservation and survival of the species. Well-maintained space boundaries make us feel protected and safe. They also serve as an advance warning system, giving us time to think or act if the need arises. Equally important, our space boundaries provide us with a predictable environment in which we can function successfully, free from jarring external surprises and intrusions.

Just as interpersonal and perceptual boundaries protect the physical area in which we operate, time-role boundaries enable us to switch roles during the day without slipping into utter chaos. Most of us cycle through a variety of roles—professional, parent, friend, lover, child, playmate, and more—in the span of 24 hours. One way to keep sane with all these changes is through the use of time boundaries assigned to various roles. We set the alarm clock to go off when it is time to wake up—marking the start of our daily roles. We know when it is time to get the kids to school (parent role), time to leave for work (professional role), time to go home (parent/spouse role), and so on. Throughout the day, people set internal expectations of what they will be doing and what will be expected of them, which helps maintain time-defined roles.

Since people cannot assume more than one role at a time, they are accustomed to switching from one role to another. They expect to switch between certain roles within a particular time frame, which makes such transitions easier. But even those expected switches can be stressful.

The most difficult and disruptive kind of role switching comes when we are caught by surprise. For example, we do not typically expect to play out certain roles, such as professional and parent, at the same time, so they do not make for an easy back-and-forth transition. That's why it is so disturbing to be at work and receive a telephone call from your child's school, or to be at home and get a call from your boss.

People have a clear need for their role boundaries to be respected if they are to maneuver successfully through their complex lives. For their sanity and productivity, they need as much control as possible over how they allocate time and roles. This control allows them to define the expectable environment—what they will be doing, and who gets to have them when.

All the while people are trying to set and defend time and space boundaries, they are striving to form a clear sense of themselves and their identity boundaries. For optimal psychological fitness, this self-knowledge must include the following: what you are and are not, your strengths and limitations, what you can and can't do, what you do and don't like, what you do and don't feel, and what you do and don't need. The more certain our identity boundaries are, the easier it is to make choices and decisions that enhance life. Identity boundaries help you find the right friends, fulfilling work, and recreation that rejuvenates.

When people maintain secure identity boundaries, they feel complete and worthwhile. They are able to say yes to things that are good for them and refuse things that are not. But self-doubt, insecurity, and anxieties can interfere with maintaining identity boundaries. When people don't feel good about themselves or are unsure about their abilities, they feel incomplete and dissatisfied. For example, when people feel threatened, they tend to look outside of themselves for something or someone to help them feel safe and strong. Sometimes they become dependent on this outside solution and it becomes part of their identity.

Boundary Erosion, Techno-Style

The boundaries that are so essential to our mental and physical well-being are under constant assault by technology. But that's not all. Your personal space is subjected to an outright technological invasion every time you:

- ▸ Find it difficult to concentrate at work because of noises from pagers, faxes, and other electronic equipment.
- ▸ Feel your home is no longer restful due to the video games played by your children or car alarms going off in the night.
- ▸ Get a headache from too many hours spent glued to a computer monitor or television screen.

Technological "Space Invaders" are coming at people relentlessly. People hear them, see them, and touch them, but they can't avoid them. Technological Space Invaders pierce people's interpersonal and perceptual space, wreck time-role boundaries, and even shake one's sense of individuality. How are they able to do so much damage? Imagine a stranger suddenly walking up to you and stopping one foot away. You would feel frightened and shaken. Your pulse would quicken, and you would try and move away as fast as possible. A technological Space Invader may seem subtle compared to someone standing toe to toe with you, but people's reactions are similar. Because each invasion is unanticipated and catches us by surprise, it activates the beginnings of a flight or fight reaction in the nervous system by telling the body to release small amounts of adrenaline. And each new Space Invader acts like a signal to the body to start this reaction all over again.

Although any single reaction to a technological Space Invader may seem mild, over time the cumulative effect can be profound. The human nervous system goes on overload. People lose their train of thought and feel irritated and ill at ease. By the end of the day, they feel extra jumpy because their bodies have been pumped full of adrenaline. Over time this continual space invasion leaves people distractible, irritable, less able to concentrate, and threatens their productivity.

This type of invasion affects people of all ages. For example, a young man named Jason was a good student, but his grades started slipping. He complained that he couldn't study at home because there were too many distractions. We asked Jason to draw a rough picture of his study area. Then we asked him to show us where he sat in relation to his clock, computer, printer, phone, answering machine, and anything else in his or a nearby room. After examining Jason's space and its invaders, we came up with an antidote. We showed Jason how to invoke "Space Creators"— ways of enhancing space boundaries and making the environment meet your needs again. For example, we told Jason to turn off the telephone ringer. We urged him to move the answering machine into another room and to turn down the volume when he was studying.

A week later, Jason reported that his concentration was improving, but he was still distracted. We convinced him to turn his clock to the wall when he was working because he kept watching the time go by and would become tense. We told him to set the alarm if he needed to finish his work by a specific time, thereby making the clock work for him. Jason was also bothered by noise from the clothes dryer and his neighbor's stereo. His parents agreed not to use the dryer while he was working, but his neighbor wasn't so compromising. So we gave Jason some foam ear plugs.

You can adapt these Space Creators to your own circumstances. Unfortunately, it is not possible to remove all technological Space Invaders. In these cases, "Reframe the Invader." Reframing entails looking at potential Space Invaders differently and then making their presence neutral or positive, rather than negative. By doing this, you shift the experience of being controlled by something to assuming control and using the Space Invader to your advantage. To reframe, you must first be able to label a sight, sound, or object as a Space Invader. Then, think of how you can turn it into something constructive.

Traveling with Space Invaders

You will also need to figure out how to use Space Creators to tackle technological invaders that travel with you—something that is becoming more and more common. A 1996 article in *Computerworld* predicted that the number of U.S. workers using portable computers will expand from about one in five today to about one in three by the year 2000. By that time, the magazine estimated, portables will constitute 80% of primary computers. Computers aren't the only machines going in our bags. The number of subscribers for cellular phones and pagers in the United States grew by 40% in 1995 to 34 million. Analysts expect as many as 100 million wireless subscribers by the year 2002.

The increased portability of technology is creating greater opportunity for time and space intrusions. When connective technology was new and rare, time-role boundaries were respected. People thought about whether a call or page was necessary. Today, we seem to have lost the sense of urgency that should be associated with intrusion. Technology allows time and space boundaries to be assaulted, but it is people who are pushing the buttons.

Communication access technology has isolated people from context. It is important that people develop the habit of creating context in their efforts to stop boundary erosion. Without knowing what is happening at the other end, we can unknowingly intrude, thereby negatively impacting the communication. You can help create context by asking these questions before attempting to access someone:

1. Where are you calling, paging, or faxing? Are you in the same time zone?
2. Where is the receiving machine physically located? Is it in someone's office or bedroom?
3. What might the recipient be doing?

Now, think about your answers. Create the context in your mind and use this information to help you decide whether to access a person now or wait until another time.

The maddening push to be reachable and to be able to reach others will be relieved if people use "Access Control" to be selective about when, where, and how they can be reached. Access Control can be asserted in several ways. For example, just because others can contact you through your cellular phone, pager, or e-mail does not mean that you have to grant them that privilege. First and foremost, don't take access technology unless you really need it.

When you need to be connected, establish your technological access preferences together with your personal time parameters. Make it clear to coworkers, supervisors, friends, and other potential time intruders how and when they may contact you. You will need to do this for each type of access technology that you have, including pagers, cell phones, regular telephones, e-mail, and so on. If you wear a pager for emergencies only, tell those with access to that number what constitutes an emergency in your mind.

And you can use technology to help control access. For example, if you are spending an hour eating dinner with your family and then playing a game or watching television, turn off the telephone ringer and let your answering machine pick up calls. (Don't cheat and monitor the answering machine—this is just as disruptive!) You can even use your technology to publicize your boundaries. For example, the message on your answering machine, voice mail, or cellular phone system could be:

> You have reached John Smith at 123-4567. Please leave your message at the beep. If it is between 6 and 8 P.M. I am spending time with my family and will have to get back to you later in the evening or the next day.

Don't worry that people will be insulted. Most callers will be envious that you are able to set such clear time boundaries.

Controlling your impulses to phone, page, or e-mail friends, colleagues, and even strangers is just as important as establishing access boundaries. To achieve "Impulse Control," people need to remind themselves of the intrusive and disruptive effect they may have when they access someone. Before sending a fax to someone's home, or activating a person's pager, ask yourself if you really need to reach them now. Think hard about it, because you are trying to break a habit that has gotten out of control. If you do not need to reach someone immediately, use another means of communication for your message, such as leaving a voice mail for the next morning. Practice delay and repeat the following mantra: "Even though I can, I won't." You will actually find yourself calming down as you change.

Are You a Victim of Technosis?

Answer the following questions:

☐ Yes ☐ No Do you feel out of touch when you haven't checked your answering machine or voice mail in the last 12 hours?

☐ Yes ☐ No Do you feel as if you can't cook a meal without technological gadgets?

☐ Yes ☐ No Do you become upset when you can't find an ATM for quick cash?

☐ Yes ☐ No Do you have difficulty writing without sitting in front of your computer?

☐ Yes ☐ No Do you have a hard time determining when you are finished with a graphic layout?

☐ Yes ☐ No Do you feel less adequate than your highly technologized peers?

☐ Yes ☐ No Do you have difficulty remembering phone numbers because you rely upon a preprogrammed speed-dial telephone?

If you answered yes to any of these questions, you may be facing "Technosis," the ultimate identity boundary enmeshment—one between you and technology. This identity boundary invasion is more subtle than those that shatter space and time boundaries. Victims of Technosis develop an attachment to technology. It grows slowly, but before people know it, they have lost sight of where they end and technology begins. Symptoms of Technosis include overdoing work and never feeling finished, believing that faster is better, and not knowing how to function successfully without technology. Technosis is a technological symbiosis with three separate, yet related, facets, which can be experienced alone or together: the "'Can/Should' Paradox," "Technodependency," and "Machine Machismo."

"Can/Should" Paradox

Because technology allows people to do so much, they believe that if a machine can, *they* should. This is the heart of the "Can/Should" Paradox. Technology *can* do more, has more to offer, and people may never exhaust its potential. They may, however, be exhausting themselves. People have lost the ability to ask and to honestly answer such questions as, "When am I really done?" and "When have I had enough?" They feel driven and pressured by the capabilities of machines, and they exceed their own human limits or the realistic needs of the situation.

Technodependency

The quest to make technology an integral part of our lives and to use it to its absolute best advantage has lead to

Technodependency. This dependency is based on three expectations. The first expectation is that technology will be available at all times. For example, people are certain that an ATM will always be close by. When they go to a hotel, they don't doubt for a moment that there will be a phone jack for their laptop, and they expect that all airplanes will have telephones.

The second expectation is that technology allows people to function successfully. Some people seem to be unable to think unless they are sitting in front of a computer screen. Their ultimate nightmare is a hard drive crash that leaves them feeling helpless or a system problem that will not allow them to access their e-mail. People become overwhelmed and sometimes incapacitated when their technology is taken away.

The third expectation is that technology allows us to have access. Another sign of Technodependency is the intense feeling that you must check in with your technology. We invade our own space by making check-in calls to our equipment. We don't feel safe without electronic connection—even though the process is disruptive and can be irritating.

Machine Machismo

The third sign of Technosis is using technology to enhance or diminish identity. People at social gatherings and at work compare baud rates and hard drive storage space as though they are in a gym, flexing muscles. Sauntering in with a pager and cellular phone attached to the chains dangling from his jeans is the modern-day technological version of a tough guy. With what we call Machine Machismo, he proudly proclaims: "My new computer has more RAM and runs as fast as anything on the market." You can hear the power in his voice. He is telling you that he is better than you.

Technological gadgets have also evolved from being tools to becoming an integral part of people's self-image. Laptops, computerized calendars, and other mechanized accoutrements are used as wardrobe items. Without their technology, many people feel naked or incomplete.

How did this technological symbiosis—or Technosis— come about? Recall our earlier discussion about the development of the self. Through the ideal developmental process, people emerge into adulthood with such clear identity boundaries that they feel whole and safe. Unfortunately, this is the theoretical ideal and not reality. Everyday emotional traumas and strains leave people feeling vulnerable. And this vulnerability fuels insecurity and dependency.

When people feel vulnerable, whether at age two or 52, they recreate a sense of safety by merging with a stronger, protective "other." This can be anything from reaching out for a hug, to holding hands, to "losing" ourselves physically in a significant other. It is as though people have some psychological gaps in their sense of self that they are continually striving to plug up, while searching for a sense of fulfillment, wholeness, and safety.

This process explains why, for example, an overly analytical engineer who feels somewhat socially uncomfortable might fall in love with a more emotional, spontaneous mate. This mate would help the engineer feel "complete." This is all well and good in relationships, where people look for someone who fits with or complements them. People feel better about themselves in this type of relationship.

It is not good to use technology in this way. And yet, that is exactly what has come about. People think work is better if it looks nicer or is finished faster. Since technology allows them to make things prettier and do them more rapidly, people feel they are better because of technology. They have literally become attached to technology to feel more confident and self-assured. For example, technology's speed, or a person's seeming lack thereof, creates a perfect "hole" for technology to fill. It comes galloping to the rescue! Computers can work at lightning speed, and so can we when we connect. As more technology emerges, people become dependent upon it to provide what they lack. This is because humans' cognitive abilities cannot be upgraded. They can only think as fast as the neurons fire in their brains, and the firing speed of neurons has not increased since the dawn of man. But they can buy a faster computer!

Identifying with technology is not good, because it causes people to lose sight of their innate talents and skills. They lose touch with who they are and what they can do. When self-esteem is built on anything other than inherent ability, it becomes as fragile and vulnerable as a house of cards. Technology is not a good attachment object and cannot make people more than they already are. In fact, by attaching to technology, people actually feel less capable over time.

When Enough Is Enough

So, how can you recognize when a task is finished? How can you draw the line between what you can expect from a machine and what you should expect from yourself? One way to stop pushing yourself past the point of "finished" is by setting time parameters. When you get into that "is it or isn't it done?" no man's land with technology, give yourself one final hour to complete the project or task. Set an alarm clock if you need to. Then hold yourself to it. And pat yourself on the back when you finish on time. Also, stop worrying about what someone else has or what is available. If you are concerned about purchasing new equipment or additional software, ask yourself if you really need it by evaluating what the new technology will give you. If it will truly offer you something you don't have now, and you really need it, buy it. If not, pass. Remember that just because you use a tool, you do not need to have the newest or quickest.

Thinking about what you need and expect from technology will help set the stage for you to pull the plug on Technosis. Advance planning will help you become less dependent. For example, take enough money out of the bank so you won't need to access quick cash. Answer all your e-mail and phone calls before leaving the office, so that you don't have to do it from home. Doing certain things the "old-fashioned way," such as handwriting a note to a friend, will give you some distance from technology. It will also help you stay in touch with yourself.

All of this is part of retraining yourself to think and conditioning yourself to technologize differently. For example, one of our colleagues got into the habit of checking her messages too often. Even though she had her voice mail set up so she could be paged in an emergency, she called in 10 times or more a day. Every time she saw a phone, she grabbed it. The telephone became a strong visual cue. When she recognized this problem she taught herself to break this habit by asking a few simple, yet powerful questions:

"Do I really need to know now?"
"Do I really want to know now?"
"Do I really want the interruption that may occur once I know?"

She acted only if the answer to one of these questions was yes. This is the way to break any negative habit. Most habits are either visually cued, in that something you see triggers the thought, or time-cued, in that a certain time of day initiates the action. Once you identify the cue, you need to ask yourself questions that force examination of the action. This prevents an automatic response to the cue, and you regain the ability to choose.

You can reinforce the steps we've talked about by grounding yourself in reality. Take a good, hard look at some of your feelings and fears. You *can* survive a hard drive crash, you *can* live without checking your e-mail hourly, you *can* use a regular knife instead of an electric one to carve meat. Make a list of your worries, fears, and dependencies. Discuss them with a friend, colleague, or spouse and create a plan for overcoming them.

Reclaiming Your Identity

It is essential to reacquaint yourself with who and what you are. Make another list, this one of your attributes and abilities. Describe the qualities and skills you possess that make you proud of yourself. When you are finished, go through the list objectively and cross out anything related to technology. This will help you focus on the areas that are uniquely you and allow you to rebuild your identity. Recognizing, respecting, and accepting your personal limits should be part of this.

Through "Identity Reclamation" you will clarify the boundaries between you and technology. The point, as we said earlier, is to get back to a clear sense of who and what you are, what you can and cannot do, and what you need and don't need. Set limits on technology and focus on your human strengths. Soon, your sense of self, satisfaction, confidence, and self-esteem will grow stronger.

4

Reach Out and Touch Someone?

‹ ‹ ‹ ‹ ‹ ‹ ‹ › › › › › › ›

W e've presented a comical image of today's technological tough guy, with his cellular phone and pager literally attached to his hip. But there is nothing funny about the impact electronic communications is having on society. As we said in Chapter 3, this type of technology has a lot to do with the struggle many people must face to reclaim their identities and cure themselves of Technosis. Electronic communication is the great temptress of modern times. It enthralls people with its newness and variety. The plethora of communication tools are like new toys, with their neon colors and science fiction designs. And there are so many compelling, instantly gratifying, and exciting ways to communicate. But the seductive pull of these faceless forms of communication goes against the very basic human need to connect in person—to touch and be touched.

A 1995 Gallup poll found that nearly two out of every five U.S. consumers have experienced a loss of face-to-face contact due to modern communication tools. Today, families and friends stay "in touch," but rarely actually connect or see each other. Quick messages left on an answering machine may leave the listener feeling burdened with one more thing to do, or shaking his head and wondering, "Why didn't she call at work? She knew I was there." How can people develop relationships or resolve problems when they are never "live"?

It's no different at work, either. Sure, videoconferencing, for example, can be a boon. It saves the time and expense of a business trip. But what if the salesperson is more compelling in person and therefore more likely to close the deal? What if the customer is put off by the technology and thinks you don't want to take the time to meet in person?

And yet, paradoxically, because there are so many new ways to connect, people sometimes yearn for distance. They react to the overwhelming stimulation of incoming messages like so many missiles. Like trauma victims, by the end of the day, they have neither the time nor the inclination for more communication. So, they revert to sneaky late-night hit-and-run e-mails, or they return calls in off-hours, when no one is likely to pick up the phone.

Can We Talk?

The impersonal 1990s stand in stark contrast to the way people communicated a century ago. Until the late 1800s, the main form of communication was word-of-mouth. Business and personal affairs were conducted by talking to someone face-to-face. If people could not get directly in touch with someone, they had someone else deliver the message in person. As a reliable postal service emerged, people learned to substitute letters for some oral communications.

This change took time, primarily because people found it difficult to communicate without the visual cues they had grown to trust. As a result of thousands of years of oral tradition, people had become adept at watching subtle body gestures, such as the slight downward curve of someone's lips. Over time, however, people learned to successfully communicate feelings and tone with written words. Letter writing developed into an art and also caught on as a business tool. But people still preferred to connect in person whenever possible. Then came the telephone, which restored some of the communication cues that were lost in letter writing. People still couldn't see the person at the other end, but at least they could hear the voice. Skills from face-to-face communication translated to phone interaction. People's ability to assign meaning through vocal cues, such as volume, tone, and inflection, helped promote the widespread adoption of the telephone.

In the past 20 years, however, a host of new tools have pushed people further and further away from face-to-face communication and live phone conversations. Answering machines, voice mail, faxes, e-mail, and other new devices rob people of many auditory and visual cues. They also frustrate the human inclination to react when something appears to be amiss. For example, when you listen to someone's phone message and hear a catch in their voice, you can't ask the machine what's wrong.

Electronic communications also tend to leave us in a state of limbo. If a call is not returned, people wonder if a machine ate their message. When an e-mail goes unanswered, people question if it ever landed. Or they become paranoid, thinking that their electronic messages are being deliberately ignored because they have said or written something wrong, hurtful, or disturbing.

That's because very often their own messages leave a lot to be desired, tending toward brevity, impulsivity, and thoughtlessness. The bottom line is that we are missing two of the main ingredients for successful communication: connection between two people and the exchange of accurate information.

This lack of closure leaves us vulnerable to a multitude of reactions. When people believe they have not been heard, they feel incomplete. When they don't know whether their message has gotten across, they feel lost. When people believe that they have expressed a message clearly and directly, and they are met with an entirely unexpected response, they experience a blow to their sense of judgment. This leads to confusion and intense frustration. Enough of these sorts of experiences, and people can start to question their sense of reality.

Learning to Communicate

Electronic communication does meet many needs, but unless it is used wisely and with awareness of its pitfalls, it can lead to all the unpleasant and unwanted feelings and situations we've been discussing. Once people learn what healthy communication is, they will see how to adapt electronic communications to meet their needs.

Humans start communicating with the world around them at birth. They refine and expand communication skills as they mature by understanding and recognizing cues. They learn to "read" their surroundings and respond appropriately. Consider, as an example, the three-year-old who lives next door to us. One day Stevie burst in on his parents with important news. He was not yet developmentally able to read their body language—heads bent slightly down, faces grim—or to perceive the sadness in their voices. While Stevie was playing outside, his parents received a phone call telling them that a friend had died unexpectedly. Had he been able to, Stevie would have used the available cues to read the context and modify his intrusion. Instead, he proceeded impulsively, and with great self-importance, saying to his parents, "Johnny pushed me!"

Parents teach their children to become socialized to the process of communication. They shape their children's speech development from day one. While children are preverbal, parents are continually showing and naming objects. When they begin to speak, children express complex needs and desires by one and two word utterances. Parents repeatedly embellish and expand these phrases, thus modeling more and more complex language construction. For example, Johnny says "Milk," and his mother says, "Oh, you'd like some milk to drink now." As children become more proficient in their word usage, parents and teachers continually help improve their pronunciation and language choices. Through the use of demonstration, repetition, encouragement, and praise, children come to be effective communicators.

Children learn not only about themselves, but about others as well. Both are necessary for successful communication. We teach them to become aware of their feelings and needs and to learn to talk about them. We teach them to think before they speak. We sometimes tell them to say nothing at all if they do not have something nice to say.

Honesty, timing, and presentation style—what linguists call pragmatics—are the communication tools children need to learn early on. As they grow, children are taught more complex pragmatics such as the ability to read physical posture, facial cues, voice tone, pitch, and intonation. These guidelines help children learn to appraise a situation and reflect on it before taking action. Children learn much of this by watching adults. They learn to become adept at assessing not only their needs, but also the context of situations and other people's needs. Most importantly, they learn to use this information to assure the best outcome for their communication.

Successful communication also requires having confidence that a message has been both expressed and heard, thereby creating a fully completed loop. The loop starts with the message you send to another person. Their reaction to you may or may not complete the loop. If you feel satisfied that their response meets your expectation and that they have accurately interpreted your message, you are done. If, however, you recognize a need to expand, clarify, or offer additional information, on you go. You use visual, auditory, and physical cues to aid in your understanding and in your being understood. When completed, a successful communication leaves you feeling satisfied and enriched.

There are "Five Cs" for successfully completing the communication loop: connection, content, context, congruence, and completion. Here is a description of how they work to form a successful communication:

- *Connection.* First and foremost, we need to connect. Unless you can access the person with whom you wish to communicate, it doesn't happen.
- *Content.* Once you have a connection, the content of the message you wish to communicate is critical. For your message to be fully understood, it needs to be detailed enough to convey all relevant aspects of the question or situation.
- *Context.* Each message needs a setting and a context. The setting should include the time of day and location from which the message is sent and where it is received. What the recipient is doing when a message arrives is also part of the communication context. Most subtly, when dealing with someone in person, communication context includes cues such as facial expressions and tone of voice. Both parties' moods, availability, and attitudes are also contextual cues. Even the weather contributes important con-

textual information for a communication. From these signs and more, people can determine a good time for communication and the best approach to take. People also use context to make sense of the response they receive.

► *Congruence.* This is the match between content and context. For a communication that leaves little or no room for misinterpretation, there needs to be a high degree of congruence. For example, if someone says, "I love you" with an earnest tone and a warm smile, the message is highly congruent. It will be believed, and the content will have been successfully communicated. If, however, the same words (content) are delivered with a sharp, sarcastic tone (context), the congruence is absent and the message can be taken in a number of ways. Honesty and self-awareness, coupled with accurate assessment and appreciation of the context, leads to congruent communication.

► *Completion.* The response you receive, along with any necessary additional exchange for clarification or discussion, leads to completion of the communication loop. You have gone full circle when all of your content has been acknowledged and you receive a comprehensive response.

Electronic communication has led to more miscommunication than ever before. Because of the absence of rules and cues, people have been using their new communication tools with only partial success. And this compounds TechnoStress.

Techno-Communication Etiquette

Now that you know what you need for successful communication, it is time to develop some rules of the road. Newer forms of electronic communication, as well as old reliable ones such as telephones and answering machines, need new guidelines for effective use.

Here are a few tips to upgrade communication etiquette:

- *Be precise.* To avoid continual "telephone tag" when trying to reach someone, make sure to say whether you will call back, or if it is their turn to reach you. If the ball is in their court, leave information about how, where, and when you can be reached. We recommend giving time ranges over a number of days.

- *Pay attention to yourself.* If it bothers you to leave messages telling people when they can get to you, consider your desire to stay disconnected. If you hang up when you reach a live voice because you only wanted to leave a message, or if you call someone's office after hours in order to get their voice mail, think about what is going on. Does it only happen with certain people, or do you feel this way all the time? What does it mean about your relationships with the people with whom you don't want to connect live? Technology has afforded people the opportunity for "pseudo-connection," or "as if" relating. You seem as though you are communicating, when in fact you really do not want to connect. We urge you to think, ponder, and perhaps work to become reacquainted with the rewards of connecting to people, not machines. Remember, it is the connection that starts the communication loop.

▸ *Get real.* We never seem to get a real person on the other end of a telephone anymore. We simply enter a world of automated options, accessible by pressing different numbers. Don't passively accept this! Press "0" for an operator if that is an option to get a real person on the line.

▸ *Know your options.* Many voice mail systems automatically page people as telephone messages are received. Some pagers actually provide digital displays of messages so the user can read them and decide what to do. Other systems don't send to pagers, or do so only if a message is marked urgent. Familiarize yourself with the systems of people with whom you connect, to know whether they get message instantly or if you must do something extra when you really need to connect immediately.

▸ *Save data.* Before deleting voice mail or e-mail from someone new, make an accurate record of their phone number or mailing address. We recommend saving the messages until you successfully connect.

▸ *Help your neighbor.* Everyone makes occasional mistakes when dialing phone numbers. If someone reaches you through a misdial, don't just hang up. Tell them they have dialed incorrectly to avoid additional call backs from the same person.

▸ *Move on.* Even with the best efforts, sometimes you can't connect. Users turn in their pagers and cellular phones, or the numbers are changed. If you absolutely can't connect with someone, don't take it personally.

Nor should you take as a personal affront the abbreviated, often clipped tone of electronic communications. The very nature of electronic communication leads us to condense our thoughts and shrink-wrap our messages. This can be interpreted as rude or abrupt. People learn to speak rapidly into answering machines and voice-mail systems through experience, because they don't know how long they have before they will be cut off. E-mails are succinct and to the point, because people know firsthand how irritating it is to scroll through dozens of lengthy messages.

The K.I.S.S. Principle

The style for electronic communication is based upon the "K.I.S.S." Principle: *K*eep *I*t *S*hort and *S*imple. Because of the volume of e-mail (ever find your name on an electronic mailing list?), calls, and pages many people receive, application of the K.I.S.S. Principle to content is understandable. All information that is delivered electronically seems to follow this principle. Even our news is condensed. Radio delivers one-minute traffic reports. Television packs so many stories into an hour-long newscast that each is only briefly covered. And now, through e-mail, you can have your news summarized and delivered twice a day. You can be paged during the day with short summaries of breaking news or you can have a ticker-tape scroll live news across your computer screen.

Condensation is impacting our ability to understand and to correctly respond to the whole picture. Here are some tips to help you around this:

▸ *Begin at the end.* Don't race at the end of any electronically recorded message. Since people don't typically know when they will be cut off, they race to leave a message until, achieving warp speed, they garble the information and forget to leave a name or number. Even after replaying, many messages are unintelligible and, therefore, unreturnable. Reverse the process. Start every message with your name, number, and the best times to reach you. You should even leave your number for people who have it, because it may not be accessible when they get your message, or they may have lost it.

▸ *Repeat yourself.* If you leave a lengthy message, you may need to recap the high points at the end. If you structure your message and offer clear direction, you stand a better chance of having your needs met. Rehearse. Not all people have the ability to think on their feet. Meandering messages are evidence of that. Many people become anxious when they have to leave a message and experience "recorder performance anxiety." Before leaving a message electronically, take time to write some notes or think about what you want to say. You will come across more clearly, calmly, and completely. Taking time to organize your thoughts also applies to written communication. Resist the urge to quickly scribble a cover note to a fax or to send a reactive e-mail.

▶ *Be fully informed.* Do not assume complete knowledge from a summary. Maintain personal responsibility for what you learn and believe. Whenever you need a complete picture, take the time to do research and be fully informed. Never make decisions or form opinions on anything less.

▶ *Be cautious.* In any communication, especially electronic, do not take the written word as gospel. Electronic communication offers a cloak of anonymity. People can be anyone or anything they want to be, and it is easy to obtain misinformation from them. This is especially true of discussion or chat groups on the Internet. Unless you do your homework, you do not have any proof of the person's credentials or the validity of the information they give you.

Combating Incongruence

With old-fashioned forms of communication, it was easier to judge the value of a source and the information provided. When one caught wind of something that didn't seem right (incongruence), one could ask questions that would help to gauge timing and clarify the context of a situation. For example, a person might say to someone, "I can't tell by your tone if you are joking" or "Is this a good time to talk?" and immediately get more context. The additional information would reestablish the congruence. E-mail, voice mail, faxes, and on-line discussions are so new that people have only begun to appreciate how they interfere with congruent communication.

When people are not afforded a total picture because of lack of congruent information, they tend to complete it themselves. As more and more contextual cues are removed from our communication, people fill in the blanks. This enables them to feel they are relating to a "whole." What one assigns to the blank spots, usually the unspoken feelings, is one's belief about what is actually there. A person may inadvertently project their own feelings into the gaps. These projections are rarely accurate, but electronic communication allows people to indulge in this tendency to their heart's content. And so, misunderstandings and misperceptions become more and more prevalent. "Why were you so short and tense when you left that voice-mail message? Did I do something to upset you?" Now they need to have more communication to clear up the previous communication. And if people don't take the time to communicate about the communication, they may harbor misconceptions and hurt feelings, which can damage relationships.

Today, professional and personal relationships can be established with people we never actually meet. This can lead to the ultimate in incongruence. Without really knowing them in person, how can we hope to fill in the blanks? With only the sound of their voice on the phone, or the quality of their e-mailed words, what can people rely on to make judgments about a person? Here are some strategies for fostering more congruent communication:

▶ *Provide cues.* Offer context as you go along. To do this well, you need to be aware of yourself and how you communicate moods by the tone of your voice or the written word. For example, if you are having a bad day and know it is apparent in your tone, but you need to leave a group voice mail message for your staff, you could alert them to your mood. You might say, "Don't read anything into my tone; it has nothing to do with you" before or at the end of your message. If you are upset with someone, tell them with words as well as tone. Say something like, "I am a little irritated about the fact that you. . . ." But if there is a problem, don't let your entire communication be electronic. Be sure to let the other person know that you will be happy to speak with them in person or on the telephone. If you are in a playful mood and are joking or teasing, make sure you say that, too.

▶ *"Emoticate."* The development of "emoticons" is an attempt to fill in the on-line context gap. Emoticons are typed symbols that can be used to indicate feelings. For example, some people leave the sign <g> to show that they are grinning, or would be if they were actually speaking the message "live." Other on-line communicators use a colon, a dash, and a right parenthesis separated by spaces like this : -) to indicate that they are smiling (lean your head sideways to the left. . . . See it?). Here are some other popular emoticons and their translations: : - (shows that someone is sad or frowning; : - o for yelling; ; -) for winking; and its companion ; - (for crying. You can use these technological creations, or you can just write what you are feeling in words. The point is to give the reader a sense of your mood, so that along with your words, they can get a congruent picture.

▶ *Ask questions.* When you are unsure of someone's mood, tone, or intent, don't assume. ASK. This is extremely important, given people's tendency to fill in the blanks. Write, call, or fax back, then wait until you have completed the picture with accurate information before forming opinions or making decisions.

▶ *Go face-to-face.* When having a long-distance work or personal relationship with someone you may never meet, fax or mail your picture and ask them to do the same. Most newer fax machines have a photo setting and make magnificent replicas of black and white photographs. This provides you with a sense of the person, and you can invoke a mental image of them when you communicate.

▶ *Good manners are a must.* Given the multitude of opportunities for incongruence, strive for optimal courtesy, tact, and thoughtfulness at all times in your messages. This way, you may head off problems on the receiving end.

Incompletion versus Completion and the Demand for Speed

The many different ways to communicate create the opportunity for more incomplete communication than ever before. Unless a person responds, you can never be certain they really received your message, fax, or e-mail. And even when they do respond, the answer may be incomplete. You may fax someone three questions, but only get an answer to one. Or you may receive an e-mail that only partially deals with the issues addressed in your original communication. When people talk live, they can say, "You haven't given me the answer to my first question." But with electronic communication, all they can do is try again.

Adding to the proliferation of incomplete electronic communication is the implicit demand for speed. Electronic communication fosters an environment in which people send only partial messages or responses. When information comes rapidly, people often feel compelled and pressured to respond in kind. But speed is not always a good thing.

For example, successful negotiations are often best conducted over time and in person. Personal relationships need time to grow. High-pressured, fast interchanges cheat everyone out of an opportunity to think, process, and make clear-headed decisions.

Take a few minutes to answer these questions: Do you have to return every e-mail you receive? How often do you check your voice mail? Do you feel compelled to answer every message and feel guilty or worried if you don't? Does an e-mail have less or more immediacy than a fax? Must you respond to a fax right away, or can it be added to your stack of "to do" papers? If a person hasn't read your urgent e-mail message, is he responsible for not attending to the issues you raised?

Since there are no rule books for new forms of communication, people attach their own meaning and importance to the various modalities. However, your rules may not match someone else's, which leads to loads of incomplete communication and TechnoStress. Try these tips to create mutual understanding and communication completion:

► *Match modes.* We use the term "Modality Matching" to describe the need to let others know the best way to reach us. Tell others how you want to be reached and what you do and don't do with certain communication technologies. If someone asks for your e-mail address, but you don't go on-line often, tell them it is not the best way to reach you. State your preference.

► *Set rules.* Along with Modality Matching, people sometimes need to communicate how they experience information sent along different routes. For example, it you take a fax as a demand to respond quickly, tell others not to fax you unless it is an emergency.

► *Give deadlines.* Provide deadlines for responding if timeliness is important to you. This is part of the structure and guidance needed for successfully completing the loop. We suggest giving yourself a little extra time in case you don't hear back before your deadline. That way, you still have time to contact the person again.

► *Back yourself up.* Even knowing someone's preferred modality does not ensure they will receive an important message within your time frame. If you need someone to read a fax or e-mail right away, it might be in your best interest to leave them a phone message letting them know you've sent them important information.

▸ *Try, try again.* If you don't get a needed response, don't give up or feel like you are a nuisance. Keep trying. Remember, your electronic communication may not have landed.

▸ *If you get lost in cyberspace. . . .* Most messages sent from one person to another on the same on-line service are trackable. But, unfortunately, most e-mail messages are not. If an e-mail message is incorrectly addressed or the person no longer has an e-mail account with that particular service, the message will usually get bounced back to you with a message such as: "MESSAGE DELIVERY ERROR—NO SUCH USERNAME." When this happens, you have to resort to calling the person to get their new e-mail address or deliver your message directly.

▸ *Don't assume privacy.* Just because you send someone a message doesn't mean that they receive it personally. We have met executives who "don't do e-mail" but want to look computer literate, so they include an e-mail address on their business card. A secretary or assistant reads and screens the e-mail and prints out important messages. If you need to know that your message has been read personally, say so. Ask for an e-mail confirmation to be sent to you stating that the message has been received and what will happen next.

▸ *Take notes.* Just as you want to organize your thoughts before composing a message, you should also take notes while listening to voice mail. If someone's tone offends you, don't react quickly out of anger. Take time to ponder your response. Make sure your response covers all the issues that are raised. With e-mail, it may at times be best to print out a hard copy, think through your response, and compose a draft. Sometimes, it is wise to have someone edit your draft before it is sent.

► *Strive for personal contact.* Don't always use electronic communications just because you can or because you are responding to a message received electronically. If your message or reply is complex or requires interaction, it may be better to deliver it live, either by phone or in person.

► *Make choices.* If you become burdened by the chore of reading or responding to electronic communication, filter your responses. Not all messages need to be listened to or dealt with immediately. Take control of your electronic communication by deciding when and how to respond.

► *Avoid junk mail.* There are thousands of Internet discussion groups and chat rooms. Anyone with on-line access can join a special interest discussion group. Comments are exchanged via e-mail. Some discussion groups are very active, showering subscribers with hundreds of messages per day. If you join such a group and feel burdened by the volume of e-mail, you have options. Many discussion groups have archives, which let you read descriptive titles and request the messages you want to read. And you always have the option of dropping your membership in the discussion group.

By using the tips we have given, you will ensure communication success and complete the loop. Now let's take an even deeper look at the growing area of on-line communication and the unique dilemmas it brings.

On-Line Communication

An ever-increasing segment of our population is going on-line. The number of Internet users is nearly doubling annually. According to a 1997 Salomon Brothers report, it will grow from about 35 million to 160 million worldwide by the year 2000. Being on-line carries tremendous promise and a handful of possible pitfalls. With awareness and alertness, you can overcome the perils, and on-line communication can remain a valuable part of the communication array at your disposal.

One of the potential pitfalls is the rapid closeness that can develop between people who meet on-line. Discussion groups and chat rooms seemingly allow us to get to know each other quickly. The way people relate can spiral into a rapid exchange of increasingly more intimate, self-revealing messages. They begin to feel close, needed. They belong. But to what? We eagerly rush to check our e-mail, wondering what the delivery will bring. If people become caught up in this spiral, they rarely ask how their e-mail friends came to take such a prominent place in their lives. They just continue to send more messages.

There is a strong, seductive pull to an on-line relationship. We can be anyone we want to be. We can try on different identities, and no one can hold us accountable for our actions. Unlike "real life," where people have learned not to rush a new friendship by phoning or seeing someone too often, on-line it seems permissible to fire off message after message without any qualms. It is not unusual for people to exchange self-revealing messages several times a day. People can go from being strangers to feeling like soul mates in a matter of hours.

Due to their own needs and desires, people begin to invest their new "cyber-friend" with a complex psychological tapestry of their own design. And though they may feel they have found a soul mate, they've only entered into a psychologically created, projected dream.

Roger, one of our clients, developed a network of on-line friendships across the United States. He had been corresponding with one woman for quite some time when the idea of the two of them traveling to meet face-to-face was raised. Roger eagerly planned this get-together.

But when he returned, Roger was disenchanted and dismayed. He had not felt at all what he expected to feel meeting this person. Even though their on-line communications had been filled with spontaneous, rich humor, support, and understanding, conversation during their weekend was often stilted and difficult to maintain. They seemed to have little in common, and Roger felt very confused. He couldn't understand how this could happen after they'd been corresponding for months.

Relationships take time to develop, because we need to get to know what we like and don't like in people. This is the way friends are made in real life. On-line you see only what another person chooses to put forward, and it may not be real, honest, or complete. Of course, not all on-line relationships involve romantic liaisons. For example, a 1996 study by Malcolm Parks, professor of speech communication at the University of Washington, found that while nearly two-thirds of those he studied had formed personal relationships on-line, only 8% were romantic in nature. The rest were friendships.

The ability to connect at any time in cyberspace also promotes a feeling of closeness. Want a friend at 4 A.M.? Go on-line and visit a chat room. There is always someone who wants to talk. Want to send a message to your new e-mail friend? You can do it anytime and from anywhere. It is exciting to feel this connected.

In addition to accessibility, on-line communication also fosters emotional disclosure. The experience of relating on-line is akin to a "Techno-Confessional." A person is in front of a screen, instead of beside one. Wrapped in a protective shell of a faceless, voiceless world, one can easily purge one's soul to trusted strangers. On the flip side, messages can just as easily be aggressive and biting. Ask an innocent question in an on-line discussion group, and you may receive dozens of replies, some helpful and others downright insulting. In the extreme, this is called being flamed and it is akin to being yelled at on-line. In the real world, as opposed to the virtual world, people are rarely this rude or confrontational—because there could be dangerous consequences. In the safe confines of the on-line world, people can indulge their aggressive impulses, without fear of physical repercussions.

Many people are drawn to on-line communication by its extremely compelling nature. Sherry Turkle, an MIT professor considered by many to be the Margaret Mead of cyberspace, describes on-line "holding power" in her 1984 book, *The Second Self: Computers and the Human Spirit*. This power enraptures the user and ensnares him in a dimension that has no sense of time. Hours feel like minutes. Anyone who has been on-line has probably experienced this. You log on just to check your e-mail or to briefly visit a chat group, and the next time you look at the clock, hours have passed. This is holding power!

Developing an On-Line Ego

Why are people so different on-line? Sigmund Freud, the founder of psychoanalysis, postulated that each person has three internal personality components that regulate behavior—the id, the ego, and the superego. The id represents our most basic and unrefined drives. Operating strictly from instinctual needs, the id is impulsive, sexual, and aggressive. According to Freud, the id obeys the "pleasure principle" by seeking immediate gratification for its needs. It does not think of consequences; it wants what it wants NOW!

The superego holds the rules. It embodies our sense of right and wrong. First from our parents, and then on through our development, our superego learns, refines, and comes to guide our successful interactions with others. It helps us know right from wrong. It is our conscience.

The ego is the overriding, executive force that keeps us on course. The ego works from the "reality principle," finding a way to meet our needs within the context of a given situation. Through maturity, the ego harnesses the id's storehouse of energy and is able to use its fuel to propel us into satisfying love relationships, meeting our professional goals, and achieving a life of fulfillment. Utilizing the superego's code of conduct as a guideline to keep behavior appropriate, the ego helps us withstand distress and experience love and joy.

During electronic communication, mature, fully functioning, and thoughtful adults are thrown into a developmental backslide by technology. They regress to an earlier stage and act from their untamed, unrefined parts. They become impulsive, sending e-mail messages with abandon. They can be whoever they want to be. They can say anything they like. Because they can, they do.

On-line comments become more aggressive as people feel a freedom to share irritation or outrage and use profanity. They wear sexuality on their sleeves. They flirt, share intimacies, become quickly attached, and give themselves provocative "handles," or names. They fall in love or in lust with ease. For some on-line communicators, there is no well-defined sense of taking responsibility for their actions.

On-line communication is the most contextless form of connecting. People are taken into an unfamiliar realm where, with no established rules to follow, they function without any superego guidance. All familiar contextual cues are stripped away, and they operate without the benefit of a mature and guiding ego.

Without the ego to guide them, people find themselves relating on-line in ways we would never contemplate in real life. They might profess love to someone they have "known" for only a week. And then, if they become disenchanted and want out of the relationship, they just change their e-mail address. Being on-line allows people to do and say things they may never dream of in real life.

For this reason, people need to develop an on-line ego. Here are some tips that may help you:

- ▸ *To thine own self be true.* It is imperative that you insure your safety and security while enjoying the connectivity that on-line communication provides. Stay aware of your own feelings, be mindful of the pitfalls, and pace yourself and your on-line relationships.

- ▸ *Let it be.* Most on-line relationships need to stay just that—on-line relationships. They may meet a specific need, but generally they do not offer the necessary components of a healthy "live" relationship. Have them when they fill your needs, then let them go. Expect that they may start with a flurry and then end abruptly. This is a function of on-line relating and has nothing to do with you.

- ▸ *Chill.* Monitor your emotions and your activity level. Is what you are feeling and expressing appropriate for the situation? Are you disclosing too much too soon? Are you corresponding too frequently? Are you divulging sensitive personal information? It's okay to slow down your pace of communication.

Now You Can Complete the Loop . . . Electronically

We are drawn to electronic communication in the hopes that we will connect even better, faster, clearer, and more

efficiently. That is technology's promise. Yet there are haz-
ards to successful electronic communication that interfere
or delay the transmission of our message. As we have
shown, electronic communication interferes with each of
the Five Cs, and on-line communication brings many new
dilemmas. No wonder it has been so hard! But now, by utilizing the concrete tips we have offered, you can put your
electronic communication back on the road to success.

5

Running at Warp(ed) Speed

< < < < < < < > > > > > > >

With all of the demands and concerns being placed on society by technology, it is easy to understand why people are more stressed, harried, and rushed than ever before. In fact, a 1995 *U.S. News and World Report* poll found that 51% of the adults surveyed would rather have more time than more money.

Advanced technology has long tempted people with its time-saving properties. The promise of how it would change our lives for the better was held out at the 1964 World's Fair in New York, at an exhibit called the Carousel of Progress, sponsored by the General Electric Company. Visitors were titillated by colorful visions of how much brighter, easier, and time-efficient the future would be because of technology. And in many ways, it is.

More people are embracing today's technology to save time. But they are not using that extra time for leisure. They are running as fast as they can, moving at warp(ed) speed, juggling too many tasks, and always wondering, "Where did the time go?"

Humans, particularly in the Western world, have a love/hate relationship with time. No scientist has ever figured out how to add another hour or even a minute to our days, but that is what many of us long for. Time is the one thing we can't manufacture; the best we can do is try to get more out of the time we have by moving faster and being more efficient and productive. Consequently, we want everything else in our world to move faster.

Technology does offer tremendous time-saving opportunities. A microwave oven can heat a complete meal in seconds. An e-mail message can be sent to Germany in the time it takes to lick and seal an envelope. Coffee-makers can grind the beans and have the coffee brewed by the time we awaken. The list goes on and on.

But even though technology offers true advantages, something is wrong. Technospeed is falling short of satisfying human needs. People do things faster, but they don't feel productive. They produce more, but they don't feel in control. There are, in fact, huge discrepancies between the amount of time people save through technology and the leisure time they end up enjoying; between expectations they now have of themselves (and that others have of them) and what they actually have time to accomplish. In short, society has embraced technological advances because they promise time and, with time, control. And with control, freedom. But this technologically induced freedom is illusory. Even as technology enables us to get those speedy deliveries we think we want, people are impatient, frustrated, out of control, short on sleep and patience, physiologically overstimulated, overwhelmed, and most decidedly short on time.

What are we really after? Perhaps we gave too little thought to technology's promise. It's up to people to see technology for what it is and recognize how technology helps and harms them.

To put technology into perspective in our lives, we need to understand how we got to this technological frenzy in the first place. The explanation hinges upon time and speed. The rate at which modern technology has been introduced has had a major impact on us. Technology used to take years to develop and even longer to become part of mainstream society. This gave people time to adjust to new innovations and to change their behavior accordingly. They had time to decide if they wanted a certain technology and, if so, how it would fit into their world.

For thousands of years, the slow pace of technological innovation afforded people these practical and emotional necessities. They came, over time, to see the practicality and benefits of each major technological advancement. And because they had time to think about them, people trusted such devices as the radio, automobile, and telephone.

The importance of needing time to fully integrate technology was demonstrated in a 1995 Visa International survey, which asked Generation Xers (19- to 31-year-olds) to rate the technological achievements that had made the most difference in their lives. The top choice was the microwave oven! This was selected by 82% of the respondents. Second choice was the ATM, selected by 55%. Both of these technologies have been around awhile. Newer technologies (including the computer), not yet fully integrated into their lives, were farther down on the list.

In his 1980 book, *The Third Wave*, Alvin Toffler, a historian and futurist, described the impact of technology as a series of intersecting waves, with one set of lifestyles replaced by another, based on the next wave of technological innovation. Each wave brings with it great change—a new way of life and of viewing ourselves and the world. As one wave begins to lose energy, another starts to build. Toffler found that the greatest societal turbulence and trauma occurred during the transition when one wave (era) was waning and the next was beginning.

Each wave has been only about one-tenth as long as the preceding one, meaning that people have had less and less time to adjust. For example, Toffler's first wave spanned thousands of years, encompassing the agricultural era. The second wave took 300 years and saw the rise of industrialized civilization. The third wave—the technological era—had its beginnings in the late 1970s and should complete itself within a few decades. This means people are in the midst of a difficult transition. The fourth wave has not yet formed, but it may take society to unparalleled technologies and applications. This fourth wave will be more compressed than the third, and the fifth wave will be shorter still. It begins to feel as if the turbulence from these intersecting waves never subsides.

Already, technological momentum has increased far beyond society's current needs. Consequently, instead of eagerly awaiting the arrival of a much-touted invention, people find themselves playing catch-up with innovations they never dreamed of and often don't understand.

Despite our changed relationship with technology, people still have that residual trust they developed in simpler times. In general, they still believe that if a scientist invents something, it must be good for them and they should have it. This has led to a divergent experience of technology in the population. A few can't wait to buy and play with their next toy. Others grab it with gusto, then wonder what to do with it. Many feel intimidated, inadequate, frustrated, or alienated.

Sunrise, Sunset

Everyday life used to have very clear limits. In olden days, people awoke with the first rays of sunlight and stopped work when the sun set. Later, the kerosene lamp, then electricity, allowed greater choice. Eventually, an eight-hour workday evolved. It started at 8:00 or 9:00 in the morning, and at 5:00 or 5:30, people closed up shop and went home to dinner and family. But somewhere between General Electric's Carousel of Progress and today, that predictable lifestyle changed. People now work longer days, split shifts, double shifts, or, using technology, they work from home.

103

Technology helped facilitate this transition by showing people that they could (and, therefore, should?) test and push through the well-established workday limits. At first, this seemed exciting. But now, the problem is that doing more work has become the norm, so there is little flexibility to create more free time. The quest for additional discretionary time has been further hampered by people's inability to accurately estimate time with respect to tasks. This happened because technology changed the parameters. People tell themselves it will only take them a minute to check their e-mail—an hour later, they are still engrossed in the computer, not even aware of the passing time.

There is another by-product of this missing-time phenomenon. Because we expect and need to do everything faster to meet the demands of technology, we have become more impatient with ourselves, others, and technology. As Stephan Rechtschaffen so aptly states in his book *Time Shifting,* "We have become human doings, not human beings."

People give themselves little time to be creative, to contemplate, and to simply be. They feel pressured to get everything done as fast as possible. The efficiency afforded by technology leads people to take on more and more responsibility. All the while, their inaccurate assessments of the actual time required to complete each task are taking a toll.

The human body was not built to run 24 hours a day in a fully alert state. People need downtime for the body to recuperate from stress. Downtime is a period of reduced energy and, biochemically, decreased levels of adrenaline and noradrenaline. There is even evidence that the body cools off a half degree during sleep.

But technology may be exposing us to conditions we are not psychologically and physiologically equipped to handle. Doesn't your heart race a little when you press a wrong button and suddenly your computer screen says "Fatal error number 1112"? Do you get nervous when a complex voice mail system states, "You have 10 seconds to make your selection, or you will be disconnected." Does the clothes dryer's loud beep jar you a bit? The perceptual and physiological overstimulation people receive from technology keeps them on edge. Consequently, people need to establish limits with technology in order to regain a sense of balance and security.

What Do We Really Need from Time?

The feeling of being unable to strike a balance between technology and the time required for basic human needs is exacerbated by the inability to accurately appraise time. Whether consciously aware of it or not, people constantly supervise themselves. One part of the human intellect is always watching how and what we are doing and providing internal feedback. This part helps us evaluate and praise ourselves while critiquing areas that need improvement or change. We set self-expectations and then measure our performance against several standards, one of which is time.

We determine internally how long we think a task will take. Then, we assess how much time we have to do the task and use this information to decide whether to do it and when it will fit into our schedule. Later, we evaluate how long the task actually took compared to our expectation and, in so doing, evaluate our performance. If we finish what we thought would be a one hour job in only 40 minutes, we feel proud of our success. If we think a job should take an hour and it takes us three hours, we feel inadequate and unsuccessful—or maybe even lazy.

The desire to accomplish set tasks in what we perceive as a reasonable time frame is tied to the human need to feel productive and in control. For high self-esteem and a feeling of mastery, which people strive to achieve, men and women need to feel in charge of their destiny. Many people struggle with this throughout their lives, hoping to achieve some modicum of balance and safety, which provides a framework for control. They travel metaphysical, existential, psychotherapeutic, spiritual, and religious avenues to help them with things that seem out of their control or that are difficult to accept.

To be in charge, people need to have a sense of control over time. They need to feel able to make their own decisions about how to use time. They need to choose when to be productive and when to goof off. Having the freedom to make these choices hinges on people's ability to organize and juggle their world.

Humans are distinct among animals because they can simultaneously perform multiple mental tasks. The human mind contains a built-in filtering mechanism that allows people to focus on the task at hand, while keeping other thoughts on the "back burner" in the brain. This filter allows people to become engrossed in a novel without experiencing intrusive thoughts about what to cook for dinner or what errands need completion. Without this filter, people would be unable to keep their thoughts organized or to focus deeply on an issue with sustained attention.

Multitasking Madness

The unique ability to juggle multiple thoughts at the same time is called multitasking. Through multitasking, humans can rapidly shift their attention back and forth from one task or thought to another, which allows them, for example, to talk on the phone while watching television. The impression this creates is that people are doing both simultaneously. In reality, they attend to one for a bit, switch attention to the other, and then switch back again. If they are focusing on the television show and the person on the phone says something particularly startling, their attention will be drawn back to the conversation.

Let's take a look at how this rapid switching works. Psychologists who study brain function and information storage and retrieval describe the brain as a massive associative network of interconnected thoughts. A good way to think of this network of thoughts (which are really electrical impulses) is by visualizing a huge board of lightbulbs that are all connected by wires. Similar thoughts are grouped more closely together, while thoughts that are different are only linked through distant, tenuous wiring. When you to think of the word "apple," what comes to mind is not just an apple. You may see a red apple image in your mind, imagine the crunch as you bite into one, visualize or even smell your grandmother's fresh-baked apple pie. Some of you may hear the word apple and associate it with your Apple computer, or with other fruit, such as oranges and bananas. It is unlikely, however, that the word apple will evoke thoughts of Moby Dick or a favorite pair of shoes (unless you happened to have dropped an apple on them recently).

Using the lightbulb board analogy, when you hear the word apple, a lightbulb labeled "apple" lights up. Because this lightbulb is wired to other surrounding ones, they start to light up, too. And as they light up, so do others in the area. Your apple lightbulb is the brightest, and as you move farther away the lights get dimmer and dimmer. The Moby Dick lightbulb, way on the other side of the board, doesn't light up at all.

Now, picture a task you are doing as a lit up area on the board (or in your brain). At any given time, there are other areas lit in your brain as well. As we write this sentence, for example, not only are we thinking about the concepts we are conveying, but we can notice that the room is warm, we can hear children playing outside, and we are aware that it is lunchtime. The area on the board around writing shines brightest, while the other areas are dim. As we really concentrate on writing, the others dim even more. It actually seems as though the noises, warmth, and hunger disappear. However, should one of the children start crying outside, our awareness of her (and what she needs) will brighten, while writing momentarily falls by the wayside.

Thus, the brain's special filtering mechanism allows a person to attend to one thought, while keeping others dimly lit in its recesses. If you need to think about something else, the filter allows you to switch your attention to another area and brighten it while the other areas dim. For example, you can cook dinner, do laundry, supervise your children, and listen to the evening news, and your filter organizes it all.

Whereas technology is designed to multitask nearly infinitely, humans are not. Like jugglers, people have inherent limits as to how many balls they can keep in the air at the same time. If they try to manage too much at once, their cognitive system, or brain, doesn't work very well. In fact, with just a few too many thoughts, our entire system goes into serious overload and, just like the overextended juggler, all the balls start falling, and one must scramble to pick up the pieces. We become victims of "Multitasking Madness."

When animals are forced to multitask, they become nervous, frightened, and eventually frozen into inactivity or launched into a frenzy. Humans subjected to excessive laboratory-induced multitasking show increased tension, diminished perceived control, and even experience physical discomfort.

We believe that technology has led people to exceed their task limits. It has beguiled them into Multitasking Madness. Look around you. You'll see people everywhere talking on the telephone while walking or driving down the street. At work you'll see people reading faxes, or flipping rapidly through screens on their computer, while making a phone call. Lights are flashing all over their brains, and they are shifting focus rapidly.

Because we don't take all of this multitasking into account, most of us have become hopelessly inaccurate at estimating how long a task will take. So, when faced with a question such as, "Do you have time to do this?" we mentally (mis)calculate our available time and say, "Sure, I've got time," when in reality we don't have enough time at all. We add yet another project to the stack and, in so doing, give our brains an additional area to filter. There is more and more to juggle, and on and on we go.

One of the first signs of Multitasking Madness is when we find it difficult to concentrate on a single task for any length of time. Thoughts of other unfinished tasks or conversations keep creeping into our consciousness, as our filtering system can no longer keep intruding thoughts from grabbing our attention from one lit up associative network and dragging it to another. Our thoughts keep flitting from one to another as we become unable to coherently organize our mind.

One reason this happens is an effort on the brain's part to ensure we don't forget anything important. Surely you have experienced this. You might be working on a report or project and trying to concentrate, as a stray thought breaks your concentration, reminding you that you haven't called your mother for more than a week. Or you are playing a game with your children and start thinking about cooking dinner, until the children loudly complain, "It's your turn—you're not paying attention."

Another sign of Multitasking Madness is when you seem to be losing your memory. You walk into the bedroom and stop because you can't remember what it was you were supposed to do. You start a sentence and lose your train of thought half way through. You misspeak words or can't find the right word when you need it. You feel as if your brain has suddenly become sluggish or even stopped working. It is like peak electricity demand during a heat wave. Everyone is running air conditioners or fans, which draw lots of power. Then, when additional appliances are turned on, they take longer and longer to kick into full gear. Sometimes, just one more appliance is too much, and the circuit breaker shuts off the power.

On a deeper level, while the brain, our information processing system, is trying to juggle more than it can efficiently handle, doing the best it can switching from one thought to another, it becomes highly activated. Areas are lit up all over the board. Our filter is working overtime just to keep everything straight. At times like this, we jump at the ringing of a telephone or a sudden beep from a pager, because with so much energy being used to monitor our internal thoughts, little active attention can be paid to the outside world. Under these conditions, any external intrusion, no matter how insignificant, signals a potential problem and demands an immediate, jarring shift from internal monitoring to external focus to check out the noise.

When we are experiencing processing overload, the brain runs at full tilt at times when it really needs to be quiet and resting. So, in the middle of the night, we wake with a myriad of ideas filling our mind and are unable to fall back asleep until they are removed from our active consciousness. We are actually searching for ways to turn off our brains and get the rest we need. In his engaging book, *Sleep Thieves,* Stanley Coren makes a strong case that people are getting less sleep than they need, accumulating an eight-hour-plus weekly "sleep debt." So, under the influences of sleep deprivation and Multitasking Madness, people must function in a world where their attention is grabbed and refocused every few seconds. Is it any wonder that people have trouble sustaining internal focus? The brain and information processing system have not changed. But they are constantly pushed to their limits. On a long-term basis, this can have seriously debilitating effects.

To stop Multitasking Madness, people must first become better at estimating time, so they won't be inclined to take on too many tasks simultaneously. This involves understanding "Time Compression," which we'll talk more about later. People must also stop relying on their internal memory—the one inside their head—and develop an external memory.

An external memory is simply an object, such as a pad of paper, that allows you to create extra storage. This enables your mind to relax a bit and feel safe. Your filter gets a chance to regroup. Once this support system is in place, thoughts will cease to intrude on other thoughts. When you find your mind overloaded, write down everything that you are thinking and feeling. This "brain dump" serves a clearing and refreshing function. And it sometimes allows you to clarify thoughts that you couldn't quite put a finger on before. Carry a small pad and pen with you wherever you go, and when random thoughts intrude, write them down. People with sleeping difficulties might keep a notepad next to the bed. The simple action of jotting down intrusive, sleep-robbing thoughts actually frees your brain from having to continually alert you to them and keep you awake.

Unfinished tasks can also play havoc with an active mind. Many people who don't complete a task add it to a mental or actual "to do" list. After practicing the "Time Expansion" exercises a little further on in this chapter, you will be better able to accurately predict the time needed to complete various tasks. By undoing Multitasking Madness, you will stop adding more and more things to your lists. However, you may need to practice another, very important technique.

You will need to stop procrastinating. Retrain yourself to recognize that many tasks can be completed immediately and do not need to be added to any list. If you are a procrastinator, you are continually juggling more and more unfinished tasks. You are needlessly overstimulating and overtaxing your brain and sensory systems. If you finish tasks, you will have less to carry within your internal memory. You will feel calmer, more successful, accomplished, and proud.

If you have something to do, do it as soon as you think of it. If you can't, write it down on a schedule or "to do" list with a date that says when you will complete it. Hold yourself to this deadline. If you find that you keep moving a task ahead on your calendar, or carry it over to each new "to do" list you create, evaluate if it is really necessary. If the answer is no, or at least not at this time, drop it from your list.

Honing your powers of concentration will also enable you to focus and whittle away at tasks in an organized manner. If you find that you can't concentrate or stay very long on a single thought or idea, and you keep thinking of other things you can do, learn to concentrate. Meditation, yoga, allowing yourself to get lost in a good book, and visualization are all useful techniques to help build the ability to focus and shun distraction. Even utilizing all of these techniques, however, does not guarantee that your brain will be able to let go. It may be in such an overstimulated state that it keeps manufacturing ideas and worries.

Learning to shift focus is another way to stop the intrusion brought about by Multitasking Madness. Think of it as creating a perceptual shift to lessen overstimulation. To accomplish this, you need to become deeply involved in something that will allow you to shift focus.

For example, if your sleep remains disrupted after you have already written down all important thoughts, try turning on the light and reading, letting the escape into a good story help your brain settle out of its worry or "creative" mode and back into a restful, quiet state. This usually allows the body to release the necessary chemicals to put you back to sleep. During the day, use other activities, such as calling a friend, reading a magazine, watching a few minutes of television, or going for a walk, to shift focus.

If, after trying all of these suggestions, you still can't break out of Multitasking Madness, enlist the help of an external monitor or supervisor. Use a significant other, trusted friend, or a colleague at work who knows you well and who can tell you when to say "enough."

Avoiding Burnout

The ability to think about and perform more than one task at a time, coupled with enormous exposure to technological stimulation, can lead to burnout. As people strive to make the most of their time, they must take measures to preserve their physiological and perceptual sanity. Everywhere today, there are intrusive and overstimulating lights, noises, sounds, and images crashing into our perceptual fields. From a ringing cell phone jarring the subdued atmosphere at a restaurant to the harsh red glare of a digital display, the human body is constantly bombarded with sensory overstimulation. Our nervous systems remain perpetually excited. It's like being in a constant state of red alert.

Humans need downtime, internal peacefulness, and uninterrupted sleep. The body needs to heal, rejuvenate, and keep its immune systems operational in order to fend off illness. Without these things, people become sick, cranky, depressed, anxious, distracted, and TechnoStressed.

It's important to remember that technology is not responsible for robbing us of the ability to appraise time, or to filter and organize information and tasks. We control our actions. We control technology. Therefore, we are ultimately responsible for letting technology lull us into neglecting our needs. But we can take back control.

Where Technology Interferes with Our Needs

Technology has put time, and therefore the awareness of time, "in our face." Wherever people look today, they see a clock. And not just a clock, but a digital clock. And, more often than not, that clock not only shows the minutes clicking by, but the seconds and even hundredths of seconds as well.

At one time in history, the relative position of the sun was about the only means available to assess the passage of time. Through technological innovations, starting with the sundial and ending with analog watches, telling time became easier and more precise. Ten to 15 years ago, when someone was asked the time, they said, after looking at the hands of their watch, "about half past twelve," "almost six," or, "a few minutes after one." This imprecision reflected a relatively relaxed sense of time. Ask the time today, and many people answer in precise minutes and even seconds. This is because technology has exposed us to digital precision.

Microwave ovens, coffeemakers, VCRs, computer screens, fax machines, pagers, and telephones display the time. It is integrated into billboards and building facades. We even have a clock on the thermostat in our hall. How many digital clocks do you have in your house? Just for fun, turn off the power briefly, then turn it back on. Now, walk around and count the number of blinking clocks that need to be reset. The last time we had a power outage, we had to reset 23 clocks!

Because of this heightened awareness, people now worry about time much more than ever before. Stop to

think and you will realize how consumed we have become. Our nine-year-old son tells us to warm his French
bread and butter for exactly 23 seconds in the microwave.
And he gets upset if we do not do it for precisely that
length of time.

Technology has changed our perception of time and
altered our internal clocks. Given this continual exposure
to smaller and smaller increments of time, seconds feel
like minutes and minutes feel like hours. Called "habituation," this process is one in which constant exposure to a
certain set of stimuli over time changes our perception of
those stimuli. Periods of time that felt long when mea-
sured by changes in the sun's position now feel short because our reference is now the seconds clicking by.

Because technology has set our internal clocks to "fast
forward," we constantly make inaccurate time estimations.
How often do you say things like, "I'll be over in a few
minutes," or "I'll be right back," or "I can turn this around
in a couple of hours"? Then you find that it really takes
you much longer than anticipated to complete the task.
When people make such statements, they are not lying.
They have developed a misperception of time.

The reality is that technology *can* do things faster than
before. People, however, have their limitations. But constant exposure and habituation to the omnipresent clock,
and the tendency to measure ourselves against the speed
with which technology accomplishes tasks, causes us to
misperceive time. We have fallen victim to what we call
"Time Compression."

Time Compression is the phenomenon of estimating
the amount of time it takes to do something as a much

shorter period than it really is. People think that since technology can work quickly, so can they. They also do not take into account important parts of their time estimations. Rather than view the whole process, they only see a piece. For example, the process of writing includes time to think, outline, make notes, write, rewrite, walk away, take breaks, and think some more. It's not just time at the computer. But when people estimate, they may, for example, only key into the activity time—not the thinking time. It's as if, in the mind, tasks don't count unless they are performed on, with, or to a machine. So, when we estimate how long something will take, we focus only on the "Techno-Time"—not the rest of the process. We have forgotten how to see the big picture.

People become highly self-critical when they cannot perform a task in the time they expected. As they watch the clock slide past the expected completion time, they become frustrated and wonder what is wrong with them. They find themselves always feeling behind, rushing around, and battling a sense of failure.

Time Expansion: Resetting Your Internal Clock

Because technology has thrown internal clocks off-kilter, people need to relearn how to set realistic time expectations. One way to do this is by making a "Time Tally" chart. Take a typical day in your life and write down every task you plan to do (work, chores, entertainment, meals—

even brushing your teeth). Next to each task, write an estimate of how many minutes you expect it to take. Now, as you do each one, time yourself. Write down the starting and ending times and then calculate the total task time. Keep a running list and notice the difference between how long you expected a job to take and how long it actually took. If your estimate was off by more than 30%, you are a victim of Time Compression.

Once you've done your Time Tally, you may feel overwhelmed by how much you have taken on—especially when you realize that there are not enough hours in the day to do it all. But don't panic. Remember, you never really did have that time in the first place. Getting a handle on the problem is the first step toward change. Next, try and calculate the amount of time by which you typically underestimate, and begin building that time into your mental estimates. Now you're on the road to Time Compression recovery!

The next step in Time Compression recovery is training yourself to look at the whole picture. We call this "Forest-Trees Reversal." Remember the list of steps it takes to write something? It takes a lot longer to "write"—from beginning to end—than to merely type at a keyboard. People tend to focus only on time spent at the machine. To combat this tendency, try dividing up your next task into all its component parts. Now, give a time estimate to each of the components. You'll be surprised by how many steps there are; each may take longer than you think.

The Time Tally and Forest-Trees Reversal exercises we have outlined can help you get an idea of where your time is going and why you can't get things done with the speed of a machine. The next step in combating Techno-Time is regaining control of the machines we use.

Technological Captive Moments

We spoke earlier about the human need to be the master of one's fate and to feel in control of one's environment. With this in mind, think about how you feel when you are doing the following:

- ► Waiting for the VCR to rewind a tape you need to return to the video store.
- ► Waiting for your microwave oven to finish popping a bag of popcorn.
- ► Waiting for a fax machine to finish printing out an eight-page document.
- ► Waiting behind three other cars to get to the drive-through food window.
- ► Waiting while your e-mail boots up, connects, sends, and receives messages and is finally ready for you.

Many people become impatient when they must wait for something. They drum their fingers, pace, and feel frustrated and irritated. Welcome to "Technologically Captive Moments," the experience of feeling held captive by the very devices used to save time. Technologically Captive Moments can range from a few seconds to many minutes, during which activity on your part is not actually required, yet you feel forced to wait until the technology (or person using the technology) has completed the job. This flies in the face of the human need to be productive and useful.

Television commercials created one of the original Technologically Captive Moments. At first, people were entertained by commercials, but when the novelty wore off, viewers learned to use this time to grab a snack, make a quick call, or shift the clothes from the washer into the dryer. Sponsors of the television programs realized that some people weren't watching their commercials. If viewers weren't watching, they weren't buying advertised products. So, they shortened commercials and now air them at irregular intervals. In essence, sponsors have tricked us back into watching commercials.

In addition to ever-present commercials, people's lives are becoming more and more burdened with Technologically Captive Moments. These range from the pause in word processing as an incoming e-mail arrives to being placed "on hold" and listening to Muzak. At the end of a day filled with these tiny tortures, men and women are oversensitized to wasted time and are ready to snap. Their nerves are frayed to the point where any wait, whether at a grocery store or an ATM, becomes unbearable.

As a result, people feel stressed, irritated, and angry at their fast equipment—which counterintuitively now wastes their time. Our upset spills over into how we view others in any situation in which we are forced to wait. We become irritated at the pace of the supermarket checker, even though she is using the scanning machine rather than keying the prices by hand. We get angry at the driver in front of us if he slows down to make a turn.

What is the solution? Faster technology? If you buy a faster computer and it can quickly download pictures off the Web, surely you will feel less captive? No. As we saw in the phenomenon of Time Compression, within a short period, you will habituate to this exposure of time, and it will once again feel too long. Faster technology is not the answer.

The solution to this problem lies inside each of us. Because people allow captive time to be stressful and unproductive, negative attitudes and perceptions develop. What we call "Minute Minders" can help people reclaim Technologically Captive Moments. To use Minute Minders successfully, think about those little things you would love to finish, but somehow never find time for. These Minute Minders may be anything from reading the comics, to browsing through magazines, to writing personal letters.

Next, think about your environment at home, at work, and any other place you go where you may be held technologically captive. Keep a stack of Minute Minders close by. This way, when you're waiting for your computer to boot up, or you're languishing on hold, you will be able to make use of that time. You will not believe how many articles can be skimmed or how easily Saturday night's dinner can be planned while you are waiting for an image to be downloaded from the Internet. Even traffic jams can be turned into opportunities if you keep a notepad or other Minute Minder handy. Taking a book to the car wash and reading while waiting makes this a restful experience. Over time, you will relabel captive time and come to appreciate these opportunities to finish things you never found time for before.

Another way to make the most of captive time is by using "Stress Busters." Practice relaxation, deep breathing, isometrics, or shoulder rolls. Close your eyes and visualize yourself in a favorite place. While stuck in traffic, look out the window and daydream. Really look at the flowers. Allow some peace into your day.

6

Two Kids, a Dog, and a Computer

‹ ‹ ‹ ‹ ‹ ‹ ‹ › › › › › › ›

Much of the technology that enables people to be organized and efficient at work also helps them to manage the tasks and the people vying for attention in most homes. Technology brings order (with its inherent sense of control), which, in turn, helps reduce Multitasking Madness. It may also give a person some precious downtime. Sophisticated, and relatively inexpensive, voice mail systems provide separate mailboxes for each family member, codes to keep messages private, and a paging function for emergencies. Programmable thermostats heat or cool the house just before you arrive, saving energy and money. Handheld video games and headset radios keep children occupied for hours. You can even awaken to freshly brewed coffee thanks to computerized coffee-makers.

The computer also assists today's family. Personal finances can be organized easily, and bill paying can be reduced from hours to a few minutes with a single computer program. CD-ROM encyclopedias make it a snap to find information for school reports. Faraway relatives can stay in easy contact through electronic mail. The World Wide Web offers an abundance of information. If you have a medical condition, there are many people on the Internet who will write to you offering support, along with countless medical resources.

It seems as though technology offers the family a host of benefits, without any downside, but this is an illusion. Our friend Pam recently realized that her home (and family) had been taken over by technology. Her seven-year-old son, Jimmy, was staring at the television while clutching his Nintendo joystick, bending it this way and that. Sarah, her 14-year-old daughter, was talking with a friend on her cellular phone while checking her e-mail messages on-line. Pam was deciding how long to set her microwave to cook a frozen chicken dinner. And, as soon as her husband walked through the door, she knew he would run upstairs to check his stocks on the Internet. "Here we are," Pam thought. "The family of the 90s! We're all in different rooms, each hooked up to our own techno-gadgets."

More and more families are becoming like Pam's. We are in the midst of a technologically aided erosion of the family system. Too many families are spending "together time" separately, and technology is playing a large part in this division.

Technological Isolation

Technology did not suddenly appear in our homes and push us apart overnight. This pattern has been developing over the past few generations. Think back to when technology was first introduced into the home. The first radios and television sets were causes for family celebration. If you were first on your street to have one, neighbors were invited over to listen or watch. Each night, when shows were broadcast, the entire family would gather around to enjoy an evening's entertainment—together. Episodes were discussed, issues were debated, and each week's offerings brought heightened anticipation.

Over time, however, we allowed technology to muscle in on family time. Remember TV trays? Instead of sitting around a table at dinner and conversing, these collapsible one-person tables were designed so people could eat dinner while watching the television. Conversation was not allowed when the television was on. If you had something to say, you had to speak during a commercial. People began losing their ability to be together and communicate. They started scheduling their lives around the television program guide, not family needs.

The next step in the isolation process came when the price of televisions dropped drastically and they became available in smaller sizes. A little portable television could now be placed on the kitchen counter, and another could fit nicely on the workbench in the garage. TVs were placed in every bedroom. Doors were kept closed so the sound of a laugh track on a youngster's favorite program would not interfere with the show that Mom and Dad were watching in the next room. Adult America learned to fall asleep to Johnny Carson.

The Consumer Electronics Manufacturers Association publishes periodic reports on the "household penetration of consumer electronics," summarizing how many homes own various electronic devices. Today, the average U.S. household has 3.4 television sets, and American children view more than 23 hours of television a week. Teens are not far behind, logging 21 to 22 hours per week. That's more than three hours per day. And adults are watching as much as seven hours per day. Estimates are that by the time our children graduate from high school, they will have spent more hours watching television than being in school. By retirement age, they will have spent 7 to 10 years of their lives watching television. The remote control created a couch potato nirvana. And just when many devotees thought it couldn't get any better, along came satellite dishes, delivering hundred of shows on dozens of stations. Channel surfing became a national pastime.

This same isolating pattern is emerging with other forms of technology. More than 80% of American homes have a VCR, and nearly two-thirds have a telephone answering machine, cable TV, stereo system, and cordless telephone. Not far behind are video games, and compact disc (CD) players. Telephones, stereo systems, and computers are transitioning from a single machine shared by the whole family to multiple units. Kids have their own phones and answering machines in their bedrooms. Teenagers close their doors and listen to blaring CDs or watch their favorite soap operas, taped on the VCR while they were at school.

From Couch Potato to Techno-Cocoon

Then there is the PC—personal computer. According to a 1996 Dataquest study, more than one in three U.S. homes has a PC, but the computer is not being used equally by all family members. The main users of the family computer are children. In fact, a 1995 American Learning Household survey found that 80% of family PC buyers cited their children's education as the primary motivation for their purchase. Children are certainly using those PCs, but not necessarily for educational purposes. Research by the Times Mirror Center shows that children use computers to play games more often than for any other purpose. That considered, a 1996 Microsoft survey found that 50% of the 6- to 11-year-old children who entered an annual contest sponsored by the company used computers more than two hours a day.

Some parents wonder if it's better for children to be computer users than couch potatoes. The answer is yes and no. Television watching is a passive activity. You can change the channel, but you don't control the content being broadcast. Also, it is easily shared with others. Computers, on the other hand, are interactive, and you, the user, are in control. When you interact with a computer, whether it is to play a game, surf the Net, or do homework, you are an active participant. You press the keys to change what you see and do.

The home computer envelopes the user in "Techno-Cocoon." Because computer use is interactive, the user becomes much more engrossed in the process. Losing track of time is easy because the holding power of the computer is great. Since the parents bought the computer to help their children, and since many adults are not nearly as computer-literate as youngsters, they tend to keep their distance and let the children be responsible for their own computer use. They don't interrupt or join the process, and they are unwittingly isolated from their kids by the PC.

While the kids are surfing the Net and playing computer games, some parents are longing for family togetherness. A nationwide 1996 Robert Half International survey revealed that two-thirds of Americans would cut their work hours to be able to spend more time with their family. However, simply being at home would not solve the problem. First, they would have to pry their children's fingers off the keyboard, avert their eyes from the multimedia screen displays, and disconnect pagers, cell phones, and other techno-toys. Everyone would need to be pried from their Techno-Cocoons.

Clearly, this would not be an easy task. Consider these statistics from a 1996 survey of over 3,000 visitors to a traveling Smithsonian exhibit in Los Angeles:

▶ 99% of Americans born after 1971 had used a computer before the age of 10. Of those born before 1971, only 7% had used a computer before the age of 10.

▶ More than 66% of those under age 25 called themselves intermediate, expert, or power users. Only 19% of those older than 25 rated themselves as computer literate.

Whether through on-line addiction or other forms of technological dependence, there is serious potential for family system deterioration. Children internalize and model the aggression they see on television, their computer, and video games. Technology can contribute to classroom failure. Some husbands and wives are getting their social needs met on-line rather than by their spouses. Advice columnist Ann Landers reports receiving over 50 letters a week from women and men who seek advice about leaving their spouse for someone they met on-line. Family members are isolated from one another and are forgetting how to communicate. In a society where families are under assault on a variety of fronts, technology can add to the strain.

Although we are not blaming technology for all family problems, we do believe that its proliferation exacerbates family stress. TechnoStress runs high when parents do not understand or supervise what their children are doing on-line and then suddenly discover that their kids have been corresponding with adults or visiting x-rated sites. TechnoStress is inevitable when some family members begin to dabble in cyberspace while others remain grounded on earth. Every time parents have to ask their child to do something as basic as resetting the clocks following a power outage, TechnoStress mounts. And TechnoStress is certain to rise when any family member spends family time alone in their own Techno-Cocoon, isolated and uncommunicative.

People need a healthy, well-functioning family system for support, comfort, and nurturance. Consequently, we must redefine and take charge of how and when family members use technology. It can be an asset, but only under a watchful, informed eye.

What Do Healthy Families Need?

A tremendous amount of thought and research has been dedicated to identifying what makes families work well. Based on Family Systems Theory, the study of how families function, we can distill four major needs. By maintaining these needs, families can stay healthy in the face of technology. These needs are by no means independent. They are complex and interwoven, as suggested by the "system" in Family Systems Theory. But each one is a must for a family to survive and prosper during the PC generation and beyond.

Balance between Togetherness and Separateness

First of all, families need a balance between dyadic togetherness and separateness. A family can be viewed as a set of relationships between pairs of family members, called "dyads." If the family consists of a husband and wife, the system is composed of two people, or one dyad. With a mother and father and two children, there are six dyads: Mom and Dad, Dad and oldest child, Dad and youngest child, Mom and oldest child, Mom and youngest child, and the two children.

Murray Bowen, one of the founders of Family Systems Theory, postulates that a hallmark of healthy dyadic relationship functioning is the maintenance of equilibrium and balance between two opposing forces—separateness and togetherness—between the two members of the dyad. The force toward separateness, or the need for independence, and the force toward togetherness, or the need for connection, are important counterbalancing processes at work in each relationship. Each force offsets the other.

When one member of a relationship experiences too much togetherness, he or she may desire more separateness and behave in ways that help make that happen. For example, if a husband feels a need for more separateness from his wife, he may begin to take on projects that keep him apart from her. Correspondingly, the experience of too much separateness by one person will create an increased desire for togetherness and motivate a move to increase the closeness by the other. The wife whose husband is always in the garage working on projects might start complaining that he doesn't spend enough time with her.

The forces of separateness and togetherness, and the constant movement to seek equilibrium between them, are characteristic of all human beings and their relationships. In any one dyad, whether it be between husband and wife, parent or child, or two children, one person's perception (or misperception) of lack of sufficient separation can trigger feelings of being crowded, trapped, controlled, smothered, or absorbed. Equally true is that the perception (or misperception) of lack of sufficient togetherness, or connection, can trigger feelings of being isolated, unsupported, unloved, or rejected.

Family Systems Theory points out why it is so difficult to maintain family harmony. With each pair walking the fine line between togetherness and separateness, the complexities of maintaining the proper balance are obvious. This balance becomes even more difficult as the number of members in a family grows and each person is simultaneously dealing with multiple dyadic relationships.

Family Homeostasis

In addition to balance between togetherness and separateness, families also have a need for equilibrium and belonging. To look at family functioning as a whole, rather than as a multitude of dyadic relationships, Family Systems Theory uses the principle of family homeostasis. Homeostasis, originally a term from biology, reflects the natural tendency of living organisms to seek a dynamic balance amid fluctuating conditions and relationships. When applied to families, this term explains how people function as a team, which is composed of their family members. They strive to be alert to and maintain a balance among all members' needs. Whenever there is a disruption of the family system, homeostasis serves to reestablish its balance. Through homeostasis comes a feeling of comfortable belonging and a sense of "us."

A healthy family's balancing process reveals itself in many ways. For example, Mom gives up some of her time so that she can drive her son to soccer practice three days a week. In turn, the son does the dishes so that Mom can put her feet up after dinner. If the wife comes home from work obviously upset about something, the husband sits down with her and helps her talk it through. Thus, the family develops predictable and expected patterns of communication and behavior that help maintain a balance between the needs of all family members. This feeling of belonging and the efforts to rebalance are mechanisms that help people make it through their children's adolescent years, grandparents' failing health, job changes, and a host of other intruders into the family system.

Homeostasis can create resistance to change if the change feels like a major disruption or a threat to the ongoing family function. When a family system feels unable to incorporate an event or emotion, the entire system can temporarily close down. To maintain healthy family functioning, as family members grow and change, patterns of behavior and communication must also change over time. In a healthy family, these changes are viewed as positive, providing a constant ebb and flow to the process of seeking family balance and maintaining one's sense of belonging.

Family Rules

The third need that healthy families share is the enactment of clear family rules. For healthy family functioning, there needs to be a clear understanding about power structure and role clarity—who is in charge of what, who does certain jobs, who plays what roles. Through the emergence of rules or a family ethic, families devise their own unique set of standards and expectations regarding behavior. Those in charge, and thus at the top of the family structure, establish their expectations and then teach, supervise, and discipline as necessary to maintain the standards of behavior within the family system. Family members are expected to follow these standards, or experience the agreed upon consequences if they do not. Family rules govern how people within the system define and conduct themselves.

Family rules and expectations need to develop and change as the needs of the family change and as children grow and mature. It is important that families maintain a flexibility and openness with regard to family rules and expectations. For example, while a four-year-old may be expected to make the bed by pulling up the top covers, expectations for the 14-year-old's well-made bed will be significantly different. Expectations for curfews, chores, communication patterns, and the like, will change as the family members grow and develop.

A family without rules, or a family with inflexible, unbending rules, risks serious confusion, family disharmony, and, possibly, harm to its members. Without a clear set of standards, there is no consistency. Optimally, every rule brings a useful or protective element to overall family functioning. Through the use of rules, parents teach their children how to survive and thrive in various life circumstances. Having a chain of command and consistent family standards helps each family member feel productive within the system and safe and protected from outside sources of trouble.

Continued Family Growth

Finally, families have a need to evolve. The family is like a growing, changing organism. All family members have their own independent experiences that lead to individual personal growth, while the family itself shares experiences that lead to its growth as a vital, interactive entity. When a family consists of children and adults, this process is constantly changing as the children develop. Families with preschool children will have different growth experiences than families with teenagers. Families with five children will have different growth experiences than families with only two.

Amid these varying levels of experience, a healthy family must move forward. The healthy family finds ways to share experiences, understand the differences between those at different stages of life, and balance everyone's need for personal growth on the path to continued family growth. Families who have problems sharing and balancing the needs of all members will stop growing in healthy directions. Ultimately, these families fracture and split apart as some members move forward while others resist growth and change.

The family system is truly a complicated organism that needs to grow as a unit while identifying and incorporating the changing needs of each individual. This system must simultaneously balance togetherness and separateness between each pair of members, promote belonging and system-wide balance, enhance family functioning by having clear family rules, and create continued development in its members by shared family growth. This is not an easy task! Because of the complexities inherent in successful family functioning, it is a system ripe and ready to be fractured by technology.

How Technology Interferes with Healthy Family Needs

Technology is not perceived the same way by everyone in a family system. When new technology is introduced into the family, whether it is a PC, VCR, or even a microwave oven, each member may react differently. Some may approach cautiously, even leaving it in the box for weeks, waiting for the right time to set it up, while others eagerly attack. Many new technological additions to the family unit require adjustments and accommodations from all members. Families who bring certain technology into the system without anticipating change may be beset by a host of technological perils that interfere with healthy family needs.

In a healthy family, power, structure, and rules emanate from the adults and flow to the children. A young child looks at Mom and Dad as all-knowing and all-powerful. To this young child, Mom and Dad are superheroes. Mom teaches the child to do certain things, while Dad teaches other things. With this instruction, the child develops skills and acquires the knowledge necessary to travel through the world with confidence.

While children are growing and learning, they do so in a world of rules. Very quickly they learn what is expected of them by their mom, dad, and anybody else who is part of the family. Even very young children learn how the rules differ from one adult to another and incorporate that information. That's how a three-year-old can get away with a little extra television before bed or no bath when Dad is around but won't even try doing that when Mom's in charge.

But suppose Mom and Dad buy a new VCR and, while they are struggling to understand the instruction manual, their nine-year-old son picks up the remote, presses a few buttons, and it works! Remember, children learn naturally by manipulating and playing. The son feels proud at his success, but what about the parents? What does this do to the power balance in the family? The omniscient, omnipotent parents are usurped by their child.

Now, when the family buys a personal computer, the son, who has worked on computers at school since kindergarten and who has a child's delight in learning by playing and trying things, will likely say, "I'll set it up! I can do it!" But the cautious parents may not be so sure. They wouldn't want the child to ruin the expensive computer. So, while they struggle, the child watches, offers suggestions, and is usually right, potentially to the parents' chagrin. Mom and Dad may feel inadequate, embarrassed, or ashamed. It only takes a couple of episodes, demonstrating that the child knows how to do it better and faster, for the power balance to shift. No longer is the parent the expert teaching the child; the child is now the teacher.

It only gets worse with teenagers. Teenagers believe they know everything and that parents know nothing. Parents of teenagers have always weathered this difficult phase, in part by the knowledge that the teenager's perception was often wrong. But now, when teenagers do know more about technology than the parents think they ever will, the tables are truly turned. They do know more than the parent! If parents feel unsettled by this, the power structure can become upended. And once the power structure is inverted, it can become difficult for parents to assert the family rules and expectations for their children and follow up with necessary consequences.

Even among the adults, technology can bring a shift of power. Since most families divvy up the work, consider the family in which the wife and husband each do certain chores. Suppose the wife is the one who writes the checks to pay the bills each month and the husband now decides he wants to put all the bills and financial information on a computer program. He may feel that he is being helpful, while the wife may feel that he is stepping into her territory. What if the wife doesn't want to technologize the bill paying? Is she hopelessly behind the times?

Let's say she agrees to try. We know he is excited to teach her how to pay bills by computer. But, as often happens, his teaching style does not match her learning style and they both end up tremendously frustrated. As a result of this frustration, maybe he'll start paying the bills, which is not the way the system was originally balanced. One way or the other, the balance of power can shift or turn into a struggle over who is right and who is wrong.

Our grandparents grew up in a world where a tool, whether it was kept in the kitchen or the garage, was a lifetime friend. Tools rarely broke and often were handed down from generation to generation. As people moved into the technological age, and tools acquired more moving parts, they broke more often. But, early on, most were fixable and therefore usable for a long time. Today, many tools are operated by computer chips. When they malfunction, they are not easily repaired. But people still harbor the notion that tools are invincible and that they should work for ages. They still believe in the integrity of the equipment. When technological tools cease working and can't be fixed, people are shocked, perplexed, and often experience a severe blow.

What does this do to the family system? When the VCR stops working, the microwave makes strange sounds, or the

PC's hard drive dies, the family is thrown for a loop. In Family Systems language, the family is knocked temporarily out of balance and feels threatened. It tries to rebalance amid a myriad of competing, seemingly insurmountable problems.

First, there is the issue of expense. Having to go out and purchase new equipment may severely threaten the family budget. Second, not every family member has the same level of techno-savvy, so they usually have to rely on one member's judgment about how to resolve the problem. And what if it is your child who is telling you that your computer is dead or needs more RAM?

When television entered our homes, the Federal Communications Commission established rules to make sure that adult-oriented programs would not be viewed by children. Any program that was violent or had question-able content could be shown only later in the evening when children had gone to bed. The VCR put a bit of a dent into that rule, but the PC and the Internet have made family programming impossible.

Children of any age can join a chat room on the Internet, where the content or language might be beyond their level of development. Suggestive conversations, harsh language, and flaming are common in many on-line chats. More than likely, this is shocking and disruptive to children's social savvy. We know from decades of research that when children watch violence on television and then play with other children, they become aggressive. But children can step up and, for a quarter or two, play a video game in which they karate chop and machine gun their way through the enemy. Do they really understand that this is not real life?

And then there is the World Wide Web, where thousands of sites contain material created for adults, not for the preteens who find them. Boys have long tried sneaking peeks at pornographic magazines. But on the Internet, pornography is available through a simple search.

It is not just access to sexually explicit material that may be developmentally inappropriate for children. For example, most adults do not allow their children access to their checkbook. But if you keep financial records on the computer that houses your children's games, they have access to this private information unless you specifically lock them out. Do you want your 12-year-old to know what checks you write and how you spend money? Do you want children to be able to see every letter you write on your computer? Much of what is on your computer may not be appropriate for your children's eyes.

And it is not just inappropriate use, but routine overuse of technology, that can disrupt a family system. Spending more time with technology means more time alone and less time spent with other family members. Instead of a family, you end up with a group of techno-isolated individuals. A recent survey at the University of Buffalo found that Internet users spent an average of 21 hours per week on-line. One in six spent more than 40 hours per week on the computer. Half of those surveyed said that their schoolwork or social relationships suffered because of time spent on-line. This computer addiction at school is carried over into the home.

Developing a Healthy Techno-Family System

If you feel that your family is struggling with who's in charge because the kids know so much more about technology than the adults, or if you're having trouble making and keeping rules for using technology, or if you are concerned with what children are seeing on-line, or distressed that everyone seems to be living in their own little Techno-Cocoons, don't despair. You don't have to lock up the cellular phone or throw out the PC. There are five easy ways to ensure that essential family needs are met and to develop your own healthy techno-family system. Following these steps resolves the technological perils and puts technology in its proper place—as a family asset rather than an isolating intruder.

Educate Yourself

The first step toward developing a healthy techno-family system is education. Parents need to be educated in the use of technology in order to understand what is going on in their homes. This will also create safety and stability at home. Just as we need to know our children's friends, we need to know what our children are doing on-line and with whom. Parents won't be able to ask informed questions without having some knowledge themselves. Parents need to maintain the power base and authority regarding technology in the home, and power and authority begin with knowledge.

Start at school. Ask teachers what your children are being taught about technology. But don't simply accept the school's approach. Make sure they offer your children the education and protection you want by having teachers develop an "Acceptable Use Policy" or AUP. An AUP is a legal document that spells out the following:

1. *A brief description for parents of what uses will be made of school computers.* If Internet access and e-mail are part of the curriculum, the AUP should provide a brief summary of these tools and indicate what they are and how, when, why, and by whom they will be used.

2. *An overview of potential dangers from objectionable material.* This section of an AUP covers the types of material that are accessible, yet unacceptable for children and what forms of monitoring will be used to avoid problems and exposure.

3. *A list of acceptable and unacceptable behaviors when using computers.* This should include expectations of how students should treat equipment and each other, along with what they can and can't do on school equipment.

4. *"Netiquette".* This section should detail how students are expected to conduct themselves when interacting with others on-line.

5. *Consequences of violations.* This section spells out what will happen to students who violate the terms of the AUP, ranging from verbal and written warnings to suspension.

6. *Signed agreement.* The AUP should be sent home and returned to school with the signatures of parents and their children before any computer activity begins.

Once your children's needs are met, it's your turn. Many schools are creating classes for parents, using school computers for training. Approach the principal or parent-teacher association for information. Computer companies are also helping parents learn about technology. Microsoft, for example, started a Family Technology Night program, through which parents are taught how to buy the right computer and how to help the family learn technology together. Ask your child's school if there are similar programs in your area.

Supervise and Stay Alert

The second step is to stay alert and to supervise. Arming yourself with knowledge will make it easier for you to observe your child's behavior. We strongly recommend that computers not be used behind closed doors. If the children have a computer in their room, you need to feel free to walk in at any time and see what they are doing. You should be able to sit and observe how your child is using the computer.

Be alert for any of the following warning signs of potential problems:

1. Getting less sleep than normal because of staying up late and/or waking early to be on the computer.

2. Staying home "sick" from school more often than normal.

3. Busy telephone lines when you are away from home, but the children are there.

4. Large credit-card bills for on-line service time and/or large telephone bills for connecting to a service.

5. Constantly talking about on-line friends whom you have never met.

6. Trying to cover the computer screen when you walk by or quickly changing the screen when you ask what they are doing.

7. Lots of e-mail messages every day. This could signal potentially questionable on-line relationships.

8. Lots of computer disks showing up all the time with new games and programs.

Any of these signs could indicate that your child or an adult family member is using technology to excess. Be mindful of the supreme holding power of technology. Overuse can spring up literally overnight. It doesn't take a long time to become addicted.

Family Technology Rules

The third step is to create family rules for technology. We strongly recommend the development of family rules about technological use by family members. These rules should apply in the home, at school, at a friend's house, and even at work! And they should apply equally to all family members. Although these ideas are more heavily weighted toward computers and on-line activity, each concept can and should be expanded to any technology in the home that is creating TechnoStress among family members. The following topics are important to cover in your rules:

1. *Set time limits on the use of equipment for every member of the family.* These will vary depending upon the age of the user and reason for use. You can use this idea for everything from television watching to playing video games to on-line interaction. Use a buzzer to signal a two-minute warning so the person can finish what he or she is doing. And follow up! Don't let the two-minute warning period slip by without making sure the person has stopped. Technology quickly eats away two minutes.

2. *Guarantee equal time and opportunities for each family member.* It is very important to keep in mind the age and developmental needs of each family member. Since many software programs and video games are geared toward boys, it is easy to believe that the computer is the province of your boys, and not your girls. Parents need to encourage and balance personal interactions among friends and family. This allows technology to be an asset rather than to warp development and encourage isolation.

3. *Make a conscious decision about where to put equipment.* Can you put a computer in the den, where the whole family has equal access and can explore it to-

gether? If the computer needs to be in a bedroom or office, an open-door policy is a must.

4. *Decide who has access to technology, when, and why.* We believe technology can be a great enticement to complete homework or chores. Just like a good rental movie is a special treat, surfing the Internet or playing a favorite video game can be a reward for good behavior. Make conscious choices with clear rationales.

5. *Make sure you have developmentally appropriate programs and learning tools for each family member.* There are excellent educational computer programs for children that can keep them entertained while teaching them at the same time.

6. *Share time with your children while they are using technology.* Sure, kids often want to be alone when they are playing with the computer or a video game, but every so often, sit with them and talk to them about what they are doing. Children like to show off their artwork as they are creating it on a computer. They love to brag about their latest score on a pinball game. Sit with them at the machine. Surf the Web together. Listen to what they say, and respect and appreciate their skills and knowledge. In so doing, you will be able to learn what is so attractive to them about technology.

7. *Don't think of technology as a baby-sitter.* People tend to overdo this. Technology can be a great asset, but it is not healthy for you or your family if its use is not balanced with other activities.

8. *Set rules and limits on inappropriate technology.* Just as you would not let your children watch an X-rated movie, questionable areas of technology need to be totally off-limits or explored together and discussed. There are ways to block access to adult-oriented material on all on-line services. Call the services to which you subscribe and ask how to do this. There are also computer programs that will block out sites on the World Wide Web that may be inappropriate for children.

9. *Safety needs are foremost.* All users of on-line tools need to be taught not to trust people they can't see. The importance of this lesson cannot be underestimated. The invisibility of on-line communication allows people to pose as anything they want. Children need to be taught appropriate rules to handle possible interactions. The National Center for Missing and Exploited Children has developed a list called "My Rules for On-line Safety." This list is available in their free pamphlet on *Child Safety on the Information Highway.* To obtain this valuable resource, contact the Center at 800-843-5678.

10. *Talk about technological experiences.* Your children will be exposed to sexualized content, cusswords, aggression, and more if they are allowed complete access to what is available on-line. If and when one of these situations occur, discuss the experience with your children. Treat this no differently than any other upsetting situation by letting them talk it out with you

and then making plans to prevent it from happening in the future. Try to give them context for why it happened. This is the same as you should do if you needed to explain a mugging or burglary to your child.

Family Pow-Wows

Step four is maintaining family balance and belonging. Family "Pow-Wows" are a good forum for discussing rules, problems, and experiences with technology. A Family Pow-Wow is a time when everyone in the family sits together and talks. We think it works best if everyone sits on the floor so that adults and children are all at the same level, with no television or radio on in the background. Use this time to discuss and modify, or make new family rules. Talk about what everyone is doing with technology and make the Family Pow-Wow a safe time to talk about feelings. You could address such questions as: Do we think Dad is on the computer too much? Is Johnny watching too much television? Is Susie always on the phone? Are we doing enough together on-line and as a family away from technology? What topic do we want to search this Saturday?

It is also important to use this time as an opportunity to talk about what your children and their friends have experienced on-line. And Family Pow-Wows are a great time to discuss what new technology the family might need or want. Let the kids tell you what technology their friends have, so you can discuss why you may or may not want it for your family.

Continued Growth and Exploration

The fifth and final step is to facilitate family growth and exploration. Before we purchased our dog, we narrowed the choice down to a couple of breeds. One Saturday morning, our whole family gathered around the computer and searched for information about these dogs. It was great fun. We sent e-mail questions to several experts. We downloaded some terrific dog-training tips, too, which led to some discussion about what a new puppy would be like in our household. For several days, we all went together to the computer to see which of our e-mails had been answered, and then we discussed the responses.

We encourage active involvement and family experimentation with technology. Program the VCR together. Surf the Internet as a family. Read CD-ROM encyclopedia entries together. Work on a Spanish tutorial program. Have your children teach you what they are learning in school or have discovered on their own. Show your pride in their accomplishments and grow with them. Continue to purchase age and educationally appropriate software. These are tremendous learning tools. By developing a healthy techno-family ethic, you will overcome technology's perils and keep the family's emotional needs in mind.

Today's Technological Opportunities

When your techno-family system is in place, technology can be a real asset. It offers incredible educational opportunities for everyone in the family. Whatever you want to learn, there is a computer program to teach it. Whether your teenager is preparing for the Scholastic Aptitude Test (SAT), your four-year-old is learning early reading skills, you need to write a resume, or your whole family wants to learn sign language, you can do it on your computer. And most of these programs are entertaining, educationally sound, and reasonably priced. If you are not familiar with the vast array of computer programs, go to a computer superstore—but leave your checkbook and credit cards at home. Give yourself an hour or so and just browse through the programs. We think you will be amazed.

In addition to programs you can buy, the informational resources on the Internet are extensive. And you can print hard copies of the information you desire. Take advantage of what is on-line, but always keep in mind that the information is only as good as the source.

Technology also helps you stay current. For a small monthly fee, companies will store information about your interests and send you current articles concerning them. There are also thousands of on-line discussion groups where you can read what other people think about any topic, from hobbies to movie stars. And, if you like the challenge of games, you can play hundreds of them with people all over the world.

Technology can be an asset in the management of your home environment and daily life. Smart houses know to turn on lights when you enter a room and turn them off when you leave. Programmable thermostats and lighting systems can be set to suit your needs. You can make your own travel reservations, read movie reviews, shop, browse bookstores, and take college courses on-line.

Although there is a dark side to on-line connectivity, there are also many advantages. So take time to develop your techno-family system and then enjoy the fruits of your labor.

7

Who's Really Running Your Small Business or Home Office?

‹ ‹ ‹ ‹ ‹ ‹ ‹ › › › › › › ›

What we are seeing is . . . a move from the industrial age to the information age, from a situation where we once worked together to a new realization that, with new technology, we can work anywhere. The nature of work is such that we are blurring the boundaries.

Joanne Pratt, technology consultant
on home-based business and telecommuting.

et's shift focus now from technology at home for fun and organization to technology at home for work. As we near the twenty-first century, there are two rapidly increasing groups of independent workers—those who run small businesses and those who are employed by larger companies but who work much of the time from their car or home.

Investor's Business Daily reported in mid-1996 that experts predict that by the year 2000 half of the American workforce—or more than 60 million people—will do some home-based work. Of these home-based workers, the U.S. Department of Transportation estimates that 15 million will be telecommuters, people who work for a company but are based out of a home office.

Why are there suddenly so many independent workers? Because telecommuting makes good business sense. For example:

- An American Information User survey estimated that the number of telecommuters is expected to keep growing by 15% per year, with telecommuting programs at more than two-thirds of Fortune 1,000 companies.
- Studies by Pacific Bell, Traveler's Insurance, Bell Atlantic, the city of Los Angeles, and many others have shown that telecommuters are 15 to 20% more productive than comparable office workers. A study by the city of Los Angeles also showed that telecommuters take an average of five less sick days per year.

- ► Companies save between $6,000 and $11,000 or more per year on overhead expenses when an employee telecommutes.
- ► When 10% of the workforce telecommutes only one day a week, there is a decrease of 13,000 tons of pollution and a savings of 1.2 million gallons of fuel.

Telecommuting has been used by businesses for years. It gained widespread popularity in southern California due to the need to reduce traffic flow during the 1984 Summer Olympics in Los Angeles. Then, in 1994, after the Northridge earthquake and the collapse of several major freeways, many people found themselves unable to get to work in less than two hours. To alleviate this situation, many businesses equipped employees with computers and fax machines in their homes, turning them into telecommuters. Research shows that 9 out of 10 people who began telecommuting after the Northridge earthquake still do, and 74% now say they would refuse to give it up.

But telecommuters account for only part of the independent workforce. Joining the ranks of independent at-home workers are those who lost their jobs in the business mergers and downsizing of the 1990s. And many people are still pursuing the American dream of working for themselves. According to the Small Business Administration, 30% of Americans are thinking of starting their own business.

Despite the high failure rate of independent businesses, people are much more satisfied working independently than in a corporate setting. Why are people so willing to be their own boss when there is such a constant threat of failure? One reason is the freedom from the large, anonymous, political corporate life that is gained by working from home or running a small business.

There is also a great deal of independence of thought and action that comes with owning your own business or telecommuting. No one is looking over your shoulder. You get to make many of your own decisions. In addition, many independent workers have the flexibility to set their own hours and work on tasks of their own choosing. Finally, there is a sense of personal satisfaction that independent workers gain from working on their own, reveling in their success and being able to take credit for it.

Technology's Helping Hand

As Joanne Pratt, an expert who has researched tens of thousands of telecommuters and home-based business owners, so aptly put it, "With new technology we can work *anywhere*." Technology has enabled us to have offices wherever we choose. We can install a telephone, fax machine, and a computer in a spare bedroom, a corner of a room, a closet, or even a car! There is no need to rent additional space. Market research by Giga Information Group in Norwell, Massachusetts, shows that sales of new, inexpensive, multi-function machines that serve as printer, fax, copier, and scanner are booming, with expected sales of $10 billion by 1999. Two-thirds of those purchases are being made by small businesses.

Current technology enhances creativity and productivity by making what was once impossible possible. Today's technology enables products to be created, and therefore small businesses to exist, that heretofore existed only in our dreams. For example, the 1996 meeting of the National Association of Music Merchants (NAMM) reported that digital technology is reshaping the music industry. Fully half of the product categories now in existence weren't even around 25 years ago. These new product lines facilitate the introduction of new niche music businesses, as well as the expansion of existing ones.

This same trend is evidenced throughout the small business sector. IDC/Link, a New York market research firm, has been tracking small businesses and telecommuters for years. Every report from IDC shows that as personal computers have become more powerful and more affordable, the small business sector has seen tremendous growth. Without today's technology, the explosion in small business and telecommuting would not be possible.

So what's the downside? Technology isn't perfect. Machines sometimes fail. Information can be lost. Help isn't always available when you need it most. And one major system failure or repair delay can create havoc for a small business or an independent worker. Additionally, according to a 1995 MCI-Gallup nationwide study of small business owners, 46% consider themselves to be technophobic. The very thing that makes a home office possible—technology—can create major headaches, anxieties, and possibly even losses. Because of techno-reliance, independent workers experience a fair amount of TechnoStress.

Regardless of the type of business, independent workers share common requirements: professional results obtained efficiently and reliably. Staying competitive in today's marketplace demands that independent workers be technologically up-to-date. Yet with almost half of all small business owners afraid of technology, keeping up with the demands of the business world is not always an easy chore. So independent workers are faced with a paradox: Technology enables them to compete with big business, but they are not prepared psychologically to deal with that technology. The result is TechnoStress.

And what about the millions of telecommuters who work for someone else out of a car or home office? Without today's technology, their jobs would not be possible. Yet telecommuters, who rely on communication technology, must depend on technological advances to ensure that their jobs continue to function smoothly. Telecommuters are not exempt from increased stress.

One telecommuter, Scott, recounted for us some of the problems he faces. He works for a telecommunications company in Los Angeles and began telecommuting when the Northridge earthquake tripled his commute time to work. Since Scott already had a computer at home, he only needed a separate telephone line and fax machine, which his company quickly installed. At first, it was exciting to wake up in the morning and not have to commute to work. He'd make his coffee and then walk about 20 steps to his office. He was getting a tremendous amount of work done, too. And since he saved so much time by not having to fight the freeways, he didn't mind working in his home office a bit longer than he would have worked in the main office downtown.

But after the novelty wore off, Scott noticed that his work day was starting at 7:30 each morning and not ending until his wife or kids called him for dinner. And then, if he heard the fax machine beep in the evening, he would run into the office "just to check" and sometimes not reemerge until well after everyone had gone to bed.

Scott also started to feel very disconnected from his friends at the office. Sure, he received by e-mail or fax the same memos they got, but he missed the office gossip, quick lunches, and conversations he used to have with colleagues. It just wasn't the same. Every time he phoned to talk with one of the guys, they joked with him, "Scott who?"

Scott's supervisor was not so keen on the idea of his telecommuting in the first place, but it was company policy to encourage employees to give it a try. In fact, his boss even joked with Scott about how he, too, would like to go to work in his pajamas. Scott began to worry about what his boss might say when it came time for his annual review.

Other telecommuters share the same concerns as Scott:

- According to NFO Research, 37% of home PC users say that the gain in productivity by working at home comes at the expense of leisure time. They are also concerned that their managers may expect them to be available at any time of the day or night.
- Motorola's Guide to Productive Telecommuting warns that because people who telecommute are often

highly motivated, telecommuting may lead to stress and burnout, because they tend to work much longer hours at home than at the office.

So at the same time telecommuting is booming, telecommuters experience techno-angst caused by blurring boundaries between work time and downtime, isolation from familiar people, burnout, and TechnoStress. Some stresses are due directly to technology and all the problems it brings to the home setting. Other stresses are the result of having technology that allows them to stay connected from a distance. With the ability to work anywhere comes a whole new set of problems.

Techno-Facade

One problem facing us today is that technology pits its creative capabilities against that of human beings. Inexpensive computer programs can be used to make beautiful music, spectacular artwork, and professional documents with relatively little effort by the users. But is it the program that is creating the product or is it you? People can lose sight of their original inspirations in a fog of technologically created shapes, colors, and sounds.

A profound emptiness can emerge, making people feel that their contributions are minuscule compared to what technology brings to the table. You have to push the keys and make the creative choices, but when the final product is laid out, do you feel proud and fulfilled, or upstaged?

With new technology taking people farther away from the original creative process, it almost seems as though machines can even conceive original ideas. There are probably days when you figure you could just start your equipment, leave, and come back eight hours later, and the day's work would be completed.

But this can't be done. Although technology can execute an idea, human creativity and intelligence are needed from conception to completion. So how do you retain a sense of accomplishment and self-worth in this techno-driven world?

We recommend going "back to basics." Consider something experienced by one of our friends. Mark loves to play the guitar in his free time, because music helps him to stay balanced. He's been playing since his teens, and now, in his forties, Mark has a small sound studio in his garage with the latest computerized equipment. Over the past few years, with the help of technology, Mark has learned to create the sounds of an entire symphony orchestra while simply playing his electric guitar.

At first, he was thrilled. But after a while, Mark stopped going into his garage, because he felt that his contribution to the "orchestra" was overly simplistic and uninspired. Then Mark stopped playing the guitar. What happened to Mark, and is happening to many creative people, is that his guitar playing—a channel for his creativity—was lost in the amazing technology.

We suggested that Mark take his acoustic guitar to the park and sit for an hour and play. After only one day of strumming outdoors, Mark felt so much better that the next day he played guitar with an old friend. When we next spoke with him, he had written two new songs and was back on track. He continued spending time in his back-to-basics mode and eventually returned to his studio, with a renewed appreciation of his skills, creativity, and worth.

If you are feeling detached from your creativity, recreate an enjoyable experience without using technology and revel in your skills. When you return to using technology, remember that what you have to offer is invaluable, and without you, the technology would just sit idle.

Techno-Isolation

Loss of the traditional office environment, with its camaraderie, conversation, and support system, presents other problems for independent workers. This sense of isolation can be alleviated by creating a new support network.

An independent worker who is feeling the loss of a social and professional network should consider forming or joining a community business organization to meet people with similar interests. Many professional organizations meet monthly and provide valuable contacts in the community. They are excellent sources for finding clients and service professionals who will round out your business team.

When you meet people, get their e-mail addresses and fax numbers. Then start your own chat group. When you have a problem or concern, you can turn to these folks. If you telecommute, you can reestablish links with your office support network by doing the following:

- *Try to work in the office at least once a week.* Telecommuting works best if it is limited to three or four days per week. When you are there, make time to chat with office friends. Then keep in touch with them electronically.
- *Try to attend office social functions.* When "the gang" plans to go to lunch, try to join them. This keeps you part of the group and helps you stay informed about people and policies in the office.
- *Schedule meetings at your home.* This will give coworkers an opportunity to see that your home office looks much the same as theirs. It will also help dispel thoughts of your lounging in a robe and pajamas all day.

Keeping strong links with family and friends is also extremely important for independent workers because it is so easy to blur boundaries when you are working at home and your livelihood depends upon technology. Try setting these technology boundaries:

- Turn your garage, basement, attic, or an addition to your house into your home office, so you will be less tempted to just step into the next room and check that fax.
- Set realistic work hours and adhere to them.
- When you "go to work," dress for work. When you have finished with work for the day, change into "play" clothes. This will help you separate work time from leisure time.

- When you leave your home office, turn the sound off on all equipment and close the door. What you can't hear won't tempt you.
- When family members are going to be home while you work, agree upon signals that will indicate when you are interruptible. For example, a closed door or being on the telephone are excellent signals that you should not be interrupted.
- Make sure you take the same kind of breaks that you would if you were working outside your home. That includes going to lunch and resting your eyes and hands if you spend a lot of time at the computer.
- Make a clean transition from work to family. You don't have a long commute to shift from work to family mode. As you shut down the computer and turn off the ringers on the phone and fax, use the time to mentally turn your thoughts from work to family.
- Reward your family for putting up with your home office. You might want a regular "date night" with your spouse or periodic mini-vacations with your family.
- Replace commuting time with something other than more work—take a morning walk, really read the newspaper, or exercise at a gym.
- Get out of the office as often as possible. Eat lunch outside, even if that means in the kitchen—not at your desk. Run an errand in the afternoon for a break.
- Develop and maintain a creative outlet that is non-technological, such as cooking, art, or reading.

► Do your best to avoid the perceptual overstimulation that breeds Multitasking Madness. If you feel keyed up much of the time, have difficulty settling down when you leave your home office, or have sleeping problems, you may be experiencing sensory overload. Follow the suggestions we made in Chapter 5.

What Do Independent Workers Need for Success?

Regardless of whether you run a small business inside or outside your home or telecommute, you must fulfill four basic needs to be successful:

1. *The need to be productive.* The small businessperson needs to make money to survive, and telecommuters need to get work done to justify their position and to grow within the organization. Productivity and efficiency go hand in hand. Workers with the most effective and efficient technology may likely be the most productive.
2. *The need to stay connected.* Independent workers need to stay connected to customers, potential clients, competitors, and other professionals. Telecommuters must also stay in touch with their home office. A telephone, fax machine, e-mail address, cellular phone, voice mail system, and other technological tools help them to survive and thrive.

3. *The need to have accurate, up-to-date information.* The key to success in the business world is information. In a corporate setting, information flows freely from department to department through newsletters, newspaper clippings, magazine articles, and other sources. As an independent worker, you must find much of this information yourself. Without it, you will find yourself making decisions and developing plans based on intuition alone. Technology, with news summaries sent via e-mail, the World Wide Web, or pagers, makes it easier to keep up with information flow. Research via the Internet frees you from having to go to a library.

4. *The need for outside support.* The independent worker can't do it alone. Because you are functioning "independently," and have a less immediately accessible support network, you need extra emotional support from family, friends, and coworkers (if any) to make all the hard work worthwhile. In addition, you need professional support from technicians, consultants, printers, and others to keep your business productive.

Techno-Dependency

In a big business setting, when technological problems arise, an employee can call on the people who have been hired to deal with technological malfunctions. For independent workers, however, when the inevitable technological problems arise, they realize just how dependent upon technology they have become. Productivity stops.

The onus is on you and you alone because there is no technical support. Either you fix it or you find an outside professional to remedy the problem. This can leave you feeling techno-helpless.

Independent workers are skilled in their own areas, but they are not repair technicians, nor should they have to function as such. Many of them do not know how to cope when technology fails them. As an independent worker, you cannot avoid technological problems, but you can avoid feeling lost and helpless when they happen.

Emergency Techno-Crash Plan

For starters, you must develop your own "Emergency Techno-Crash Plan" (ETCP). Every business is required by law to have an evacuation and safety plan to deal with natural emergencies such as fires and earthquakes. We believe that as an independent worker you also need an emergency plan, one that deals with possible technological disasters. Here's how to create one, using a spread-sheet on your computer or a pad of paper:

- *ETCP Column 1: Office Technology List.* List all technological equipment involved in your work in the first column. This should include computers, communication systems (phones, fax machine, and so on), lighting and temperature controls, computer software, and technologically created information such as client files, accounts receivable, and reports.
- *ETCP Column 2: Equipment Usage.* Indicate in the next column whether you need each type of technology daily, weekly, monthly, or annually.

▶ *ETCP Column 3: Emergency Contingency.* In the final column you should decide for each piece of equipment or information what you will do *when* it stops working properly or becomes unavailable. Options include repairing or replacing the equipment.

When a problem occurs, first try to repair it yourself if you are technologically inclined. But set a clear time limit and adhere to it. If you are not successful, call a professional. High-tech equipment often requires specialized repair tools. For each piece of equipment that must be sent out for repair, keep a list of at least two to three reliable technicians. Update this list frequently by asking other independent workers for information about repair people they use. When your equipment needs repair, call each shop and ask how long it will take to fix and how much it will cost. Your choice should be based on time and expense, depending upon the urgency of the repair. Ask repair technicians if they will come to you or if you must take the equipment to them.

Some equipment that is used daily must be fixed immediately to avoid a severe loss of productivity. If you can afford it, purchase backups for each critical item, such as a printer cartridge. Keep a list of at least three to four vendors for each piece of equipment. If you don't need to replace something urgently, consider ordering it by mail, which can cut up to 30% off the price. Some mail-order suppliers will also ship overnight in an emergency. Also consider renting or leasing instead of purchasing expensive equipment.

You should also have a contingency plan for power outages. To prepare this plan, turn off the electricity while your office is in typical running condition. What happens? Do you have candles or flashlights in the office? Does your phone system still operate? When you turn the power back on, what happens to all your equipment? Do clocks need to be reset? Don't forget to check clocks on the fax machine, computer, and voice mail. Make note of all that happens and what needs to be done. Attach it to your crash plan.

Pay homage to Murphy's Law! Build in extra time when setting deadlines for projects that rely on technology. It is very important to plan time for possible problems and their solutions.

An Emergency Techno-Crash Plan takes only about an hour to develop. It should be updated at least every six months or whenever new technology is acquired. With a clear plan, you will never be caught feeling techno-helpless.

Techno-Speed Trap

Technology appropriate to the business world changes as rapidly as most other machines today. Trying to keep up creates a speed trap of sorts, which contributes to a feeling of techno-helplessness. In the corporate world, the responsibility for keeping up is usually shared by an entire staff. If you are telecommuting, all of your electronic needs should be filled by the company for which you work. But if you are a small business person, you must make your own choices about new technology—choices that may be driven by the competition as well as by basic operational needs. If potential clients speak with your competitors via e-mail, for example, then you must get e-mail, too. We think the best way to decide on what you need to keep your competitive edge is to form a new technology acquisition plan, following these five-steps:

1. Evaluate each new piece of equipment. Then ask yourself if you are productive with the technology you already have. Will the new technology make you more productive? If the answer to the first question is yes and the second is no, pass on the new product.

2. If you think you need new technology, the next step is to evaluate costs compared with benefits. Don't forget to include hidden costs, such as supplies, repair, and maintenance. Remember also that when any new technology comes on the market, it is very costly. But after it is accepted, the price usually drops. So, if you can afford to wait a while, you may get a better buy.

3. If new technology will help increase productivity and is expensive, but cost-effective, consider renting with an option to buy.

4. When purchasing new equipment, determine who will install and check it. If you assume this responsibility, set a limit on how much time you can invest. If you exceed your allotted time, hire a consultant.

5. Once the equipment is working, take the time to familiarize yourself with it. Always practice with equipment before you need to use it for work.

The Independent Worker's Technology Bill of Rights

Technology puts independent workers in the driver's seat, so to speak. But it can create such dependency that it may even lead to questioning one's own creativity and capabilities. To keep technology in it's proper perspective, declare your independence.

1. **I am the boss, not my technology.**
2. **Technology is available to help me express my creativity.**
3. **I decide when to use the tools technology provides.**
4. **I have the right to choose what technology to use and what to put aside.**
5. **I can use technology to stay connected, informed, and productive—my way.**
6. **Technology offers a world of information. I get to choose what information is important to me.**
7. **Technology will have problems, but I will be prepared to handle them.**
8. **Technology can work 24-hour days, but I can choose when to begin and when to stop working.**
9. **Technology never needs to rest, but I do.**
10. **I can work successfully by enforcing my boundary needs.**

8

Corporate TechnoStress

‹ ‹ ‹ ‹ ‹ ‹ ‹ › › › › › › ›

P eople who graduate from college today can expect to have four to six different careers before retiring. Two of those careers don't even exist now, because they involve technology that hasn't yet been invented. It is harder and harder for businesses and workers to keep up with the pace of this technological treadmill. The U.S. Department of Labor reports that more than half of all new jobs today require some form of computer literacy and that by the year 2000, 60% of new jobs will require technical skills possessed by only 22% of the workforce.

Technology is advancing on businesses at a fast and furious pace, and it is leaving a trail of TechnoStress at every level of the organization. From the employee at the lowest ladder rung to the chief executive officer at the top, corporate workers are feeling the pangs of rapidly changing technology and its effect on shaping jobs and expectations. Every day brings yet another new communication device, software program, or piece of computer hardware that workers *have* to know, *need* to use, or *must* have to do their job.

"A Computer on Every Desk"

Steven Jobs, the founder of Apple Computer, dreamed of a computer on every desk. His dream has become, for many workers, a nightmare. In fact, half of all executives, managers, and clerical workers describe themselves as TechnoStressed. Why? Some of the main problems are that workers have little control over what technology they use, little training on how to use it, and little respite from the constant stream of information and innovation.

The Technological Imperative

People have an inherent need to be in control of their environment. But new technology is often introduced without warning or employee input. We recently studied over 200 clerical workers, 300 managers, and 50 executives: 78% of those we surveyed had no input into the decision that they would use a computer. In fact, most employees have no choice about what technological tools they use.

Once the company invests in an e-mail system, it would be a breach of corporate etiquette—and a sure sign of technophobia—for the employee to use the tried and true paper memo.

New technology is usually introduced with a corporate imperative to begin using it immediately—but there is often little or no instruction on how to use it. As we discussed in Chapter 2, the learning curve for new technology is usually fairly steep. But the vast majority of the respondents to our survey ranked the training they received as ranging between "only fair" and "not so good" to "terrible." And even if employees do manage to master new technology, the process begins again as soon as the next innovation comes along. Workers who don't keep up will be left behind or, worse yet, rendered obsolete.

Judging from the tremendous number of new job categories that have shown up in the past few years—computer programmer, computer repair technician, computer support technician—the adage that computers create more jobs than they eliminate seems accurate. Look deeper, and the outlook isn't as sunny. All of these new jobs require advanced technical skills. In the face of rapidly encroaching technology, employment prospects are bleak for unskilled workers. A recent study by Canadian Research Networks found that the spread of computers in the workplace is rapidly wiping out job opportunities for the less-skilled portion of the workforce.

Employees are also looking over their shoulder to see if the latest computer-generated pink slip has their name at the top. These fears are certainly justified. In his book, *The End of Work: The Decline of the Global Labor Force and the Dawn of the Post-Market Era,* Jeremy Rifkin reports that we are entering an era in which computers, robots, and technology will replace the vast majority of workers. Rifkin gives one example of how a human bank teller can work eight hours a day and handle about 200 transactions, while an ATM can work 168 hours per week and execute 2,000 transactions a day! And all this is at about the same cost as that single employee. Between 1983 and 1993, this vast differential in efficiency cost 180,000 bank tellers their jobs.

Even if they don't lose their jobs, employees must cope with stresses technology creates. Although the few Eager Adopters in our midst revel at the arrival of every new gadget, the rest of the workforce struggles with each innovation. We asked business people what about technology made their work life so stressful. Here are the top five complaints of survey respondents:

1. System problems.
2. Computer errors.
3. The time it takes to learn new technology.
4. The reality that "time-saving" technology seems to end up requiring more work rather than less work.
5. The fact that technology is always changing too fast to keep up.

Although it didn't make the top five in our study, another rapidly growing source of techno-angst is technology-aided employee scrutiny. Under the Electronic Privacy Act of 1986, as long as an employer tells its employees they're being monitored, the organization is free to read e-mail, listen to calls, or even videotape an employee. Already, over

40 million American workers are subject to electronic surveillance through computer files, e-mail logs, and other technology. A recent *MacWorld* survey reported that 15% of the nation's companies said they listen to voice mail to monitor performance, that 42% monitor e-mail, and that 74% read computer files.

Operators who take airline reservations, sell advertising, or anyone whose job involves talking to customers on the telephone, are likely to be subjected to electronic scrutiny. Computer programs routinely monitor operators' performances to determine the number of calls they are taking per hour. In many companies, the software keeps track of what each employee is doing. Even keystrokes on the computer are monitored, one by one. Employees must log on and off their computers when they use the restroom, go to lunch, or take a break. At the touch of a button, these surveillance programs can compute the average length of an employee's lunch hour, a secretary's average typing speed, or whether a worker has made or received personal phone calls. Yet, as anyone who's ever participated in a staring contest can attest, the problem with all of this Big Brother technology is that constant scrutiny can be very disconcerting. In fact, we wouldn't be all that surprised to find that electronic surveillance plays a role in lowering employee productivity and job satisfaction.

The omnipresence of technology, time-wasting computer glitches, rapid changes in systems and machines, worries about job security, and constant techno-scrutiny has lead to generalized technological angst. And because anxiety interferes with the ability to concentrate, this

TechnoStress can make workers less productive, less efficient, and less satisfied with their jobs. It's a vicious circle.

Technological Fear and Loathing in the Boardroom

Although employees are struggling with technology, in some ways the TechnoStress is even worse in the executive suite. Management concerns are reflected in several major studies. A recent national Gallup poll sponsored by MCI found that business managers were worried that technology would lead to these problems:

► Loss of privacy.
► Information inundation.
► Erosion of face-to-face contact.
► Continually having to learn new skills.
► Being passed over for promotion because of their lack of knowledge.

How do managers and executives deal with these concerns? Many practice denial—keeping their distance from the very technology that they require employees to use.

Studies have shown that while over 80% percent of the senior managers at some of the largest corporations in the United States now have a computer on their desks, up to 50% of these executives never turn on their machines. This same MCI-Gallup poll showed that 91% of executives are not on-line, 66% don't use e-mail, 67% do not carry beepers, and less than half personally use their company's voice mail system.

This phenomenon leads to a "Techno-Generation Gap." Management makes decisions about acquiring expensive technology—yet it avoids this same technology like the plague. A study by Roper Starch Worldwide found the majority of American managers suffer from a "technical knowledge gap." Many do not even type. So how can they use a word processor or e-mail? Yet it is more than just a lack of practical or technical knowledge. The same educational issues and time pressures that make technology stressful for workers also impact managers. Many managers feel they must always be on top of things, and they aren't willing to risk losing face in front of a colleague or employee by asking how to use the new word-processing program or fax machine.

This leaves corporate management trapped between a rock and a hard place. Executives are being told by the media, consultants, their competition, and their technical staff that they need to constantly improve and update their company's technology. In fact, James Champy, author of the book *Fast Forward: The Best Ideas on Managing Business Change* says that new ideas and technologies in business are piling on so fast that it's becoming a job in itself just dealing with them. It seems that every new day in the corporate world brings a new technology. Businesses were just getting used to the idea of moving from typewriters to word processors when all of a sudden along came faxes and e-mail. Then the World Wide Web showed up. And every day, corporate leaders—many of whom aren't technologically inclined—must make critical decisions about which technology to invest in and when.

It is tough to rationalize signing off on expensive equipment purchases when you cannot gauge the extent of the advantages to be gained from the new technology—let alone judge the relative merits of the various models available. And then there is the question of providing an adequate budget for maintenance, upgrades, training, and support, when none of these important functions contribute to the bottom line. Most corporate decision makers are forced to rely upon the techno-speaking Eager Adopters on the company's Management Information System (MIS) staff. But because Eager Adopters are *always* eager to embrace new innovations, their enthusiasm needs to be tempered by the corporation's long- and short-term technological needs and goals. But the only way to get a handle on those goals is to understand the capabilities of current and emerging technologies—which leads right back to the technical knowledge gap. Another vicious circle.

Even managers who aren't victims of the knowledge gap are under a great deal of techno-duress. As soon as a new computer system is budgeted for and installed, it seems to become outmoded and obsolete. The business world had finally gotten used to all of the complex commands required in DOS when Microsoft introduced Windows, their version of the Macintosh environment, which uses pictures rather than words. For many people, just learning to use the mouse was a struggle. And just when workers adjusted to Windows, along came Windows 95. Now the business world awaits the next "revolutionary" environment, knowing full well that it will only be around for a couple of years at the most. Technology puts both employees and managers in a perpetual state of "SURPRISE"—and it is an expensive party to pay for.

The Corporate Coffers

As if worries over employee and management training are not enough, technology also strains the corporate pocketbook. According to Deloitte and Touche Consulting Group, business technology budgets increased from less than 0.5% in 1993 to 3.5% in 1994 to over 6% in 1995. Double digit budgets are imminent. American businesses are plunging increasingly larger sums of money into technology. The problem is that, often, these technological investments don't pay off in terms of increased productivity.

In many instances, the money is not even for new technology. Instead, it is spent in the hopes of alleviating unanticipated problems with current technology. Even the smartest technology often does not work as advertised or as anticipated. Business computer programs include hundreds of thousands of programming statements and are the product of an average of 12 to 18 months' work by probably a dozen or more programmers. When a program has been fully tested by the staff, it is sent out to be put through its paces by groups of people who are either currently using an earlier version of the same program or who are veteran computer users. In short, it is tested by

Eager Adopters who pretty much know how to use most any computer program. When the Eager Adopters are done finding problems, the program is then released to the public.

Immediately after a program's commercial release, software companies start a "bug file," recording the problems "typical users" encounter as they install and use the program. Not surprisingly, bug files grow rapidly, because typical users do all sorts of things to the program that its creators and testers never dreamed possible. It is not uncommon for the bug file of a large business program to contain thousands of discovered bugs in just a few short months after its release. Bugs may be a fact of life in the programming world, but they cause businesses enormous amounts of TechnoStress. A bug in a program stops productive work and then takes valuable company time to diagnose and fix. It is not a matter of just a few hours here or there. The "Year 2000" problem alone, in which many computers programmed to read years only by the last two digits (for example "98" for the year 1998) will read "00" as the year 1900 instead of 2000. This will cost companies billions of dollars to repair.

In addition to equipment and software purchases and trouble-shooting technical problems, corporations spend hundreds of millions of dollars each year keeping computers up and running. The Gartner Group reported that a typical networked PC actually costs $13,000 per year to maintain. Only 21% of that is the actual amortized cost of the hardware and software—the rest is attributable to labor costs, including administration, training, and support. And this does not even capture the cost of continually upgrading to newer, better, and faster. For, as we have seen, hardware and software can become quickly outdated due to the rapid development of new, more powerful, and more versatile technology. Once the corporate piggybank is opened, the technological costs have no end.

The Productivity Paradox

Technology promised to make business operate more smoothly, increase productivity, and free employees for more creative, interesting pursuits. In practice, instead of making business life easier, technology often has the opposite effect. Since 1980, over one trillion dollars have been invested in technology by U.S. corporations. The implicit promise was that it would make business more productive. Yet over that same time span productivity has actually dropped 1%. This confusing state of affairs has been referred to as the "productivity paradox." If you ask people in the business world how they feel technology has affected their work, as *Inc. Magazine* did, nearly all respondents will say that it has made them more productive. So, why do the facts disagree?

One reason for this paradox was uncovered in the same *Inc. Magazine* study. More than half of the participants reported that technology made their jobs more complex. In fact, a recent study by STB Accounting Systems of San Rafael, California, found that the typical PC user spends 43% of his or her time on the machine "futzing" with the computer. The downtime spent loading or changing software, organizing files, tweaking formats, or experimenting with new features doesn't translate into productivity in business terms.

Communication Overload

The other culprit in the productivity paradox is communication overload:

- ► A Yankee Group survey of 100 Fortune 1,000 companies revealed that 29% of company workforces use cellular technology, and that number is expected to grow to 53% by the end of the century.
- ► A study by the Institute for the Future found that employees of Fortune 1,000 companies send and receive 178 messages each day via communication technologies. 84% reported that their work is interrupted by messages at least 3 times an hour.
- ► Researchers at Carleton University and the University of Western Ontario studied 2,437 government employees and found that e-mail—which they considered the "killer application"—really is a killer. In fact most of the workers surveyed cited the demands placed on them via e-mail as the biggest culprit in job stress.

The same voice mail systems, fax machines, e-mails, and pagers that provide amazing connection benefits in the business world also create incredible headaches. It is not uncommon for a worker to return from lunch and find 10 new voice mail messages, 5 faxes, 18 e-mail messages, and 6 pager messages. Then that employee needs to spend an hour sorting through and responding to the messages. In the meantime, still more urgent digital missives arrive. The constant stream of incoming and outgoing messages means that businesspeople end up spending more time trying to communicate than actually doing.

If the volume of communication isn't overwhelming enough, there is the added stress engendered when every other message seems to be marked "priority." Even those messages not explicitly flagged as urgent are designed to grab our attention. From a young age, we are environmentally conditioned to go on heightened alert when certain cues, such as flashing lights, loud noises, or vibrant colors, kick in. So, it is no accident that incoming e-mail messages are announced with a loud refrain, or that Federal Express, Airborne Express, and the U.S. Postal Service use brightly colored overnight mail envelopes. All of these cues are designed to make the recipient drop what he or she is doing and attend to the incoming message. This, of course, leads to more time away from the activity (presumably the worker's regular duties) that the message interrupts.

Information Fatigue Syndrome

A 1996 Reuters Business Information study of 1,313 junior, middle, and senior business managers in the United States, England, Hong Kong, Singapore, and Australia identified a new techno-malady that they labeled "Information Fatigue Syndrome." Of those sampled, 73% felt that they needed enormous amounts of information to be successful in their job and that technology made this information more accessible. Yet at the same time, Reuters found the following:

- ▶ 33% of the managers were suffering ill health as a direct result of information overload.
- ▶ 66% percent reported that tension with work colleagues and diminished job satisfaction were directly related to the stress of information overload.
- ▶ 62% admitted that their social and personal relationships had suffered as a result of the stress of having to cope with too much information.

More than half of the managers in the Reuters study were sure that their work environment would become even more stressful over the next two years, due to the continued onslaught of information. The volume of data keeps increasing, but any clues to the value and veracity of the information have disappeared. For instance, the research department of a large corporation was asked to prepare a report on projected consumer spending trends for the next 12 months. They produced a beautiful, 100-page, four-color document with 10 pages of sources at the back and hundreds of three-dimensional graphs showing all sorts of past, current, and future data.

But a closer reading of this attractive document revealed much more flash than substance. It had the veneer of professionalism without the substance to back it up. With technology helping every step of the way, it is often difficult to judge the quality of work that has been cut-and-pasted, checked for spelling and grammar, laid out with the best of the desktop publishing tools, and enhanced by graphics that make it look like it just slid off the edge of a professional printing press. Technology not only feeds the information glut, but it also hides the clues that help managers sift through the data and make the right decisions.

The Technology-Stress Equation

Take major capital investments. Add in a technological imperative tied to a knowledge gap. Mix in a significant learning curve. Throw in a flood of communication and information. Top it all off with the false conviction that if the balance of technology is just right, the grail of dramatic productivity growth will be reached. All of these ingredients add up to a recipe for serious corporate TechnoStress. And the level of stress in the business world *has* skyrocketed in conjunction with the increasing use of technology:

- ▸ *Information Week* reported that job burnout is at an all-time high. Topping the list of burnout candidates are information systems managers and operators who are expected to keep the technology working around the clock.

- ▸ A study reported at the Fifth International Conference on Human-Computer Interaction demonstrated that computer slowdowns, breakdowns, and unavailability of correct information contribute to worker stress.

The rising stress levels have a significant price tag. It has been estimated that stress-related ailments cost U.S. corporations $300 billion per year.

Call in the Cavalry

Way back in 1984, Dr. Craig Brod warned that the way technology was implemented in most businesses "virtually guaranteed technostress." Our experience in working with a variety of businesses during the last two decades—ranging from one-person offices to multinational corporations—is that Dr. Brod was absolutely correct. Although most companies are often quite farsighted about the potential impact of technology on their business practices, we have found that they are either oblivious, in extreme denial, or incredibly naive about the impact that the technology has on the *people* who use it.

So, having embraced technology to the tune of one trillion dollars, American corporations are faced with the reality that their employees, from entry level to the presidential office, are experiencing constant and often overwhelming TechnoStress. There is no turning back from technology. It is undeniably part of our corporate world, and each day will find newer, more advanced technology showing up in our offices. So, the question is how can business introduce new technology while minimizing TechnoStress?

The solution lies in taking into account what psychology tells us about how people learn and the way they react when confronted with new things. By starting with people, it is possible to devise an effective model for integrating machines into the workplace. Our people-based model is divided into a series of 12 separate, but overlapping, phases—each of which is vital to the entire successful plan.

Phase 1: Organizational Value for Technology

We conducted a comprehensive two-year study of technological sophistication in 23 countries and found one major theme echoed by all of the countries whose citizens eagerly embraced technology. In these techno-savvy nations, technology was supported, valued, and used by decision makers at *all levels of the organization.* In technologized countries, everybody from the president on down eagerly extols the virtues of technology and models its successful and comfortable use. The president of France uses Minitel, their countrywide computer network. In Singapore, every member of the government uses e-mail. This is precisely the kind of behavior that allows for the seamless introduction of newer technologies. A certain attitude permeates this type of support: "We believe in technology and we enjoy letting it make our world easier."

Phase 2: Establish the True Need

Too often we have seen a company purchase a technology without asking the question, "Do we really need this?" Often, newer technology will not make the company any more productive, because existing technology can do the job just as well. One cautionary note here—in many instances, the question, "Do we really need this?" is posed to the wrong people. Too often it is asked only of those whose interest in the new technology has less to do with productivity than it has to do with either keeping up with others or the excitement of playing with something new. Ask everyone who will be involved. Make sure that this includes those who will actually use it.

If a need has been established for new technology, make sure that the time is invested to thoroughly investigate all the options. It is well worth the expense to talk to experts and get their opinions on what you need now and what you might need in the near future. Nobody can predict the exact future, but it makes sense to consider technology that will grow with the organization's needs. Once a need for change is determined, take time to educate employees about the rationale for the change. This will go a long way toward decreasing the inherent TechnoStress of technological change and toward increasing both worker morale and feelings of acceptance. Once the staff is on board, training needs and ongoing technical support should be factored in. As the Gartner Group study showed, only 21% of the cost of technology goes into the hardware and software. Much of the rest needs to go for administration and training.

Phase 3: Assess Staff Attitudes and Develop New Skills

We have watched corporations make a big mistake by assuming that their employees will all eagerly embrace technology. Remember our studies have shown that *more than half of all executives and managers and two-thirds of all clerical staff are either hesitant or resistant to new technology.* Before implementing technological change, find out how staff members feel about technology. This information is vital for successfully planning the rest of the process.

The technological shift over the past two decades has signaled the importance of developing new skills. Some of these are simple mechanical skills, such as typing or operating the computer mouse. Others may include understanding computer operating systems and computer problem solving. As more technology is introduced into the workplace, many employees feel that their critical thinking skills and creativity are becoming less important than their ability to operate the technology. While this shift to technology seems to provide a sense of "deskilling," or replacing human skills with computer operations, it can be presented as an opportunity for "reskilling," or learning new skills.

An organization should pay particular positive, understanding attention to any new skills required to operate technology. For example, if a vice president is going to use e-mail but he cannot type, it is imperative to provide a nonpunitive opportunity to reskill. Additionally, many forward-thinking corporations provide employees a pleasant opportunity to get used to new equipment. When one company installed computers on everyone's desk, employees were asked to play a solitaire game for a half hour of their paid workday. This gave them a nonthreatening environment to get used to the machine and keyboard, while getting paid to have fun!

Phase 4: Alleviate Technological Discomfort

Resisters and Hesitant "Prove Its" need assistance in removing their preconceived technological discomfort. Most of all, they must be told that they are not unusual or alone and that overcoming their discomfort is an important prelude to learning any new technology. Let them know it can be easily accomplished! As we stated in Chapter 1, each hesitant or resistant employee often feels that they alone experience discomfort, even though the majority of people are not Eager Adopters. Particularly in a business setting, where career advancement depends on productivity, employees are usually extremely reticent to admit what could seem to be a shortcoming.

One of the important lessons we learned from our international research was that countries where technological hesitancy and resistance were considered acceptable rather than problematic were the same countries that succeeded in getting their populace to embrace technology. Technological discomfort is not difficult to remove if an attitude of acceptance is established, bolstered by personalized education, training, and ongoing support for each employee. It is imperative that people not feel their job security is threatened or negatively judged because of their feelings, concerns, and beliefs about technology.

Phase 5: Develop Personal Motivation

In a comprehensive study of nearly 500 managers in 62 U.S. companies, Magid Igbaria from Drexel University found that "perceived usefulness" was the most critical factor in determining managers' decisions to accept or reject computer technology. This supports our view that employees must be provided with a personal motivation about the technology they are asked to use. For example, one company wanted to introduce e-mail to enhance communication. We suggested that they hold small demonstration sessions to show employees what e-mail might do for them personally. Before the demonstration, they asked each employee to find an e-mail address of a friend or colleague who did not work for their company and bring it to the session.

The session leader first showed them how to do a couple of basic e-mail operations and had them send their initial practice e-mail to a co-worker who was waiting to answer at a computer in another part of the building. Each participant was delighted to get a response just a minute or two after pushing the "send" button. That excitement was harnessed to help them send an e-mail to the person whose address they had brought. Bets were even made as to who would get the quickest response. Over the next few days responses to their outgoing e-mail came in and were posted on a bulletin board for everyone to see. As people stopped and read the messages, the growing motivation and excitement spread to the rest of the company. Needless to say, when the e-mail system was installed a month later, it was a big hit!

In our experience, before a first exposure to the World Wide Web, many resistant and hesitant users see it as useless or a time waster. So, we use this same strategy to build excitement and interest. Before we do any Web training, we ask each participant to give us a list of hobbies or other special interests. Then, in advance, we search the Web for a special site or two that offers information on each person's special interest. We make this Web page the starting point for their explorations. It never fails! Usually we have to drag people away from the computers at the end of these sessions. After this type of introduction, it is easy to show how they can make use of this tool for their business needs.

Phase 6: Increase Awareness and Support Skills in Eager Adopters

Eager Adopters can be strong allies in getting technology adopted and used successfully. First, they must recognize the negative reactions nearly everyone else is having. They need to know that not everyone else is as excited as they are about technology and do not share their joy at dealing with the inevitable computer glitches. They must come to understand and recognize the negative effect they can have on people who do not eagerly embrace technology. It is truly sad to see a computer training program effectively sabotaged by the Eager Adopter asking a question that is way over everybody else's head. You can see the hesitant and resistant people's eyes glaze over and their brains shut down. The training session is over . . . at least for them.

Most Eager Adopters willingly learn how to become understanding and considerate helpers with a little training. We meet alone with Eager Adopters and use a role-playing process, in which we play the role of a hesitant user and ask the Eager Adopter to teach us how to do something on the computer. Here's how a typical first role playing session might proceed.

Hesitant User: (played by trainer)	"Will you show me how to send an e-mail message?"
Eager Adopter:	"Sure, it's easy! All you do is boot up the computer, launch your e-mail program, pull the mail ID from your address book, compose a new message document, connect to your server and send off the message. Here, let me show you." (Eager Adopter reaches over your shoulder and rapidly presses keys for about 30 seconds and turns back to you grinning broadly.) "See how easy it is?"

At this point, the Eager Adopter has lost his trainee, which we model by staring at him blankly. Many times the Eager Adopter-trainer doesn't even notice this blank stare, and so we use stronger and stronger body language to let him know that we are "lost in cyberspace." In the most extreme cases, we have to actually stop looking at the screen and turn completely around in our chair and stare at something that is in a totally different direction from the computer.

We stop the training process and ask the Eager Adopter or any onlookers to tell us what went wrong. With a few well-chosen prompts from us, we encourage the Eager Adopters to see at least four problems:

Problem 1: Too much techno-jargon was used.
Problem 2: Too many new ideas were presented.

Problem 3: The ideas were presented too rapidly.

Problem 4: The only hands moving on the keyboard belonged to the Eager Adopter.

Next, we reverse roles, and the Eager Adopter plays the hesitant or resistant employee, while we model appropriate training techniques. We continue to do this, switching roles and modeling, until the Eager Adopter becomes a patient, understanding helper. Then, during the actual training, we can pair them up with the less techno-enthusiastic employees and the Eager Adopters become a valuable asset to our training program.

Phase 7: Involve Entire Staff in Technological Choices

A technology plan that does not allow input from the employees who will actually use the technology is doomed to resistance. Executives and end-users alike must be informed of the plan in plain language and given opportunities for questions and discussion. In his book *The Trouble with Computers,* Thomas Landauer, a University of Colorado professor, provides example after example of how the "User-Centered Design" of technology leads directly to reduced training costs, reduced human error, reduced employee turnover, increased satisfaction, and, ultimately, even new uses for the technology, which lead to even more increased productivity. User-Centered Design means that all users must be consulted about new technology, and their needs must be integrated into its design and implementation and expectations.

Phase 8: Pretest the Technology

Technology never quite works right until the bugs are worked out. Sometimes the bugs are in the technology itself, while other times they are in the entire process—training, implementation, reporting—surrounding the technology. It is imperative to pretest technology before beginning training. It is critically important to try it out with users of all Techno-Types—from Resisters to Eager Adopters—and throughout all levels of the company. Have the people testing the technology keep a log of *any* problems (technological or attitudinal) they encounter, no matter how trivial. Then use that information to solve problems with the technology or tailor the training.

When testing technology, make sure to test vendor support as well. Product manufacturer availability is particularly critical early in the implementation process. Check the following:

1. Does the vendor have telephone assistance available for questions and problems? Is it a toll-free number? Does a real person answer the phone?
2. Are the support technicians considerate on the telephone?
3. Do the support technicians talk in plain English rather than techno-speak?

Phase 9: Carefully Develop a Training Program

Based on our experience training others to use a wide variety of technology, we have distilled 16 key strategies that can be used in any training program:

1. *Limit session time.* Sessions should be short and focused.
2. *Use single concepts.* Sessions should cover a single concept at a time. The earliest ones must be practical and immediately useful.
3. *Avoid jargon.* New terms must be introduced with explanations in plain English.
4. *Use humor.* Technology training is too often an overly serious business. Research shows that humor can help with technology training, so sprinkle the sessions with relevant cartoons or observations.
5. *Use hands-on training.* Hands-on practice should be introduced early and often. It is an essential component for success. Enough equipment and time must be made available to all learners. This builds early success, motivation, and confidence.
6. *Match hardware.* Teaching on the same equipment that is to be used fosters transfer of learning more effectively.
7. *Show a variety of help tools.* Show and let learners practice using all sources of help (manual, on-line, help desk) early in the process.
8. *Match styles.* Match training to pretested levels of skills, knowledge, and psychological style.
9. *Use variety of learning styles.* Vary the teaching modality. Some people learn best through visual presentation, others through auditory channels, and still others through tactile (touch) lessons.
10. *Prepare for problems.* Computers have problems and may crash for no apparent reason. Explain this to the trainees and discuss the meaning and cure. It is amazing how many people feel that turning off the computer is not an option.

11. *Don't assume.* Don't assume any prior knowledge.

12. *Model actions.* People learn best through modeling. Have someone demonstrate first, then have the trainee perform the task, with the trainer close by for assistance.

13. *Assist, don't do.* If problems arise, the trainer should tell the trainees what to do and then let them do it. Pressing keys for someone is no help at all!

14. *Use guided exercises.* Guided exercises, with pictures of the computer screen mixed in with the text, work well with novices.

15. *Summarize often.* Summarize information frequently to solidify learning.

16. *Start early.* Make sure to train staff with lots of lead time, well before they are expected to be using the equipment. "Pressure cooker" or "need-to-know-by-yesterday" strategies are not only unsuccessful but lead to strong resentment and TechnoStress.

The trainer is a key ingredient in the training process. The trainer must understand people's adverse reactions to technology. He or she must be calm, nonevaluative and nonarrogant. It is a mistake for any trainer to say, "See, this is easy!" This will intimidate or irritate anyone who is having an uncomfortable reaction to the technology. Ongoing emotional support is also critical to training. A psychologically aware trainer will describe symptoms of discomfort at the beginning of the training and will provide learners with time to discuss these feelings and build positive coping styles. This trainer will explain potential problems and difficulties and will suggest ways of handling them psychologically as well as technically.

Phase 10: Provide Ongoing Support

In most cases, companies will also offer their own post-implementation support. Make sure to factor this into the entire process. Consider setting up a "help desk," with a physical location and a telephone staffed during business hours. Just the knowledge that help is only a phone call away is a help itself. When the help desk staff is out working on computer problems, have them carry pagers so they can return calls from frantic employees in a timely fashion.

Phase 11: Provide Ample Techno-Playtime

For years, we have been strong advocates of the importance of "play" in overcoming technological fears and developing mastery. As corroboration of this strategy, Candice Harp, a training and development consultant in Atlanta, recently did a comprehensive study of technology training methods and found that having time to experiment with the technology was rated as the top training choice. Other useful methods included asking coworkers for help and reading the on-screen help. The strategies rated as least useful included formal training seminars, lectures, demonstrations on videotape, and computer-based training courses.

Our applied research has shown that discomfort around technology does not simply depart forever. Rather, through exposure, experience, and support, the employee learns to combat any discomfort with positive coping strategies. Developing these coping mechanisms takes time! For example, after enough practice with overcoming technical glitches, an employee might learn to say internally, "This problem will be easily solved." This strategy of positive self-talk is both calming and confidence building.

Many training programs fail to include sufficient time or resources for the staff to master the material. "Techno-Playtime" must be sponsored and supported by the company and must be structured into the training and work environment without the fear of additional work pressures. There needs to be time dedicated to *explore* the technology by pushing buttons to see what happens (*and to see what bad events do not happen*). Techno-Playtime is critical to both mastering the technology and to overcoming any negative emotional responses to the technology. It enhances the learning process while providing time to practice successful coping mechanisms to deal with any discomfort. Don't expect staff to explore on their own time. Let employees know that they are *expected* to explore and play with the new system on company time. This is an important aspect of management support and a critical component of successful training.

Phase 12: Encourage, Solicit, and Integrate Staff Feedback

Throughout the process, the staff must feel comfortable providing feedback about what is making sense and what is not. A viable, successful technology-implementation program must build in time for the employees to provide feedback to trainers, managers, programmers, and support staff about their experiences with the new system. This feedback should then be incorporated into additional training to show continued system value and support.

On the Road to Technological Success

Although the above 12-phase people-centric training model will not cure every problem, it can help alleviate many of the common corporate TechnoStressors. If a business uses proper planning, awareness, and understanding, technology can realize its potential of making the business stronger and more successful, while preserving the morale and psychological and emotional well-being of the company's most important resource—its employees.

9

Our
TechnoStressed
Society

‹ ‹ ‹ ‹ ‹ ‹ ‹ › › › › › › ›

Society, as a whole, is becoming increasingly Techno-Stressed. Some stresses are subtle, but others are so prevalent that many people recognize them and experience them on a daily basis. The signs of societal Techno-Stress are evidenced, for example, in ordinary life whenever people:

► Accidentally bump into a car while walking through a parking lot, setting off an alarm that leaves them feeling like a criminal.

- ► Feel isolated by communication technologies that rarely allow them to connect to a person.
- ► Toss out new devices and equipment because they are frustrated by not being able to use them properly or because they can't repair them easily.
- ► Hear "the computer is down" as an explanation for why nobody can help them.

Technology came into our world with an implied promise that our lives would be better. The drudgery of pretechnology eras would be replaced by speed and proficiency at work and leisure time at home. Unfortunately, nobody said that we would also feel more TechnoStressed as we became "wired."

As we have said throughout this book, people are feeling technology's impact in an ever-growing spiral from their personal lives, families, and work, to how they interact with each other as human beings. Technology is no longer the territory of men in white button-down shirts and pocket protectors. It's something that we all must deal with everywhere. No single event opened the floodgates. Instead, many threads have been woven together to form societal TechnoStress.

Where Did Societal TechnoStress Come From?

How did societal TechnoStress develop? To put it simply, people became chip happy. When computer chips were bulky and cost hundreds of dollars apiece, manufacturers were not so ready to put them into anything but large computers. But when the price of making chips shrank along with their size, they started turning up everywhere. And people bought just about everything that had a digital readout: electronic fish finders, automated doggie door openers that unlock only after sensing a signal from a dog's collar, and handheld poker games. Where will it end?

The speed with which technology reinvents itself has extended into all areas of consumer automation, creating a form of built-in obsolescence in the world. Moore's Law asserts that the power of microprocessor chips doubles every 18 months and their cost is cut in half. Automated obsolescence and rapidly increasing capabilities, coupled with lowered costs, have led people to the age of disposability. Today, people devalue the old and revere the new too quickly. Why? Well, for one thing, what's old may not be fixable anymore. Or, when people try to have an electronic appliance repaired, they are told that it will cost more to fix it than to buy a new one. And the new one has so many more features, anyway. What does this teach? Today, people think nothing of replacing something old with something new, even when it is not broken!

Curiously, though, people tend not to throw away their aged or broken techno-toys. Old answering machines are stacked in the garage next to discarded coffeemakers and replaced VCRs. Computers that seemed so exciting and powerful when they arrived in the office just five years ago now gather dust in a corner of the storeroom. Sometimes this unwanted equipment is stored for parts or for backup in emergencies. But some people keep it because it cost so much, in the vain hope that their investment will pay off when the broken machine someday miraculously sputters back to life.

Not only are we technological hoarders—we've also become compulsive labelers. As technology took hold, scientific terms designating its functions became part of the commonly spoken language. Check a dictionary published prior to 1980 and compare it to one published today. The newer version contains words such as microprocessor, download, multimedia, laptop, floppy, hacker, and e-mail. No wonder many people shake their heads when they listen to techno-babble. Hundreds of these terms now pepper everyday conversations. Another byproduct of technology is that quite a few old words now have entirely new definitions. Words such as virus, bug, disk, interactive, network, paint, and mouse are just a few. "I've got a virus," your friend may tell you on the phone. How can you tell if she has the flu or if her computer is infected?

While society struggles with this new vocabulary, people are also struggling to interact with the technology it defines. Because of e-mail and the World Wide Web, society has witnessed the creation of a whole new universal language—whose letters and punctuation make no sense to most people. This strange techno-language is associated with almost every product and service available today. Want to know more about something? Contact www.productname.com. Need to talk to someone about your product? E-mail them at a similarly strange-looking address.

This rapid evolution alters the underlying social contract—the idea that there are certain fundamental principles (in this case language) that hold true always. When that underlying fabric is suddenly altered, our sense of order, justice, safety, and trust come under assault. When technology shows up unexpectedly and unannounced in heretofore familiar areas such as language, it takes us by surprise. Our sense of predictability and comfort zone of order disappear.

As a result, people are left feeling confused, irritated, frustrated, or just stupid. This leads to stress characterized by despair, hopelessness, feelings of helplessness, anger, hostility, societal rage, distrust of other people, depersonalization, immobility, and feelings of victimization.

Societal TechnoStressors

The loss of trust is having an especially strong impact on society. People do not function properly in any environment in which they feel they must constantly be on their guard, lest someone says something they can't understand, or they fall into an embarrassing technology-inspired trap at home or work. Solutions to any form of TechnoStress must start with awareness. People must understand the impact of societal TechnoStress in order to overcome it.

One form of societal TechnoStress is information overload. In an era in which the written word is so highly valued, people now find themselves being TechnoStressed by an overabundance of words. It has been estimated that information doubles in the world every 72 days. More than 2,000 books are published worldwide each day. The Library of Congress catalogs 7,000 new items every day. Thousands of new Web sites are created on a daily basis. Too much information can be as harmful as not enough.

People are being buried under this avalanche of information and the diverse nature of it. If you read five different authors on a single subject, and each disagrees with the others, who can you trust? How do you decide whose information is the most accurate? Compounding this, the public is told that people can't believe everything on the Internet because sites can be altered, and people can pretend to be knowledgeable or even expert about a subject, when in reality they are not. Where does that leave the average person? Feeling "Information TechnoStress."

A second form of societal TechnoStress is caused by isolation from human contact. People hardly ever connect with members of their own species anymore. Instead, they mostly talk to machines or computers. And e-mail and faxes are leading to the demise of the art of letter writing.

As communication modalities explode, there is a concomitant trend for people to not communicate. Messages are brief. To save time, people avoid speaking live. When busy, they purposely send calls to their voice mail. People wait to leave messages until they know the recipient will not be available to take the call.

This bobbing and weaving causes both parties to feel TechnoStressed. The person who needs to communicate, but would rather do it electronically, has the burden of avoiding contact. The receiver may feel continually frustrated trying to reach the sender, as they play the communication game of the 1990s—TechnoTag.

Individuals are not the only ones who bought into this impersonal form of communication. Many businesses rely on technology to replace person-to-person communication. Most offices have voice mail systems rather than live personnel to answer the phone. This enables companies to employ smaller staffs, but it keeps the public hanging in cyberspace. This form of communicating (or, more accurately, avoiding communicating) creates tremendous alienation.

Many doctors even use voice mail system that sound similar to this: "You have reached Dr. Smith's office. If you are a physician, please press one now. If you are calling concerning a bill, please press two. If you would like to make an appointment, please press three and someone will be with you shortly." People generally reach out to doctors when they are in need.

The impersonal nature of a voice mail systems can create a barrier between parties. It locks out live interaction and may send the message, "We might not want to speak with you. Leave a message and we'll decide later." Or, "We don't want to speak with you. Push a few buttons and do it all electronically." This leaves people feeling very alone.

To add insult to injury, many voice mail systems are difficult to follow. It's almost as if some operations purposely make their system frustrating, in the hopes that callers will give up. People reach the limits of their frustration tolerance and decide that whatever they wanted is just not worth the aggravation. They feel frustrated and without options.

Another societal stressor is caused by the ability to route communications to another location. Dial a local telephone number and, without his or her knowledge, the caller could be speaking with someone in another state. With this location-independent communication system comes the loss of accountability. When you are dealing with someone in your community, they feel more accountable to follow through and complete a job. This is because your paths may well cross in a social situation, or they may need a favor from you someday. But if you are forced to do business with someone thousands of miles away, they can have a very impersonal approach to you and your needs. New technology promised to deliver a global village—instead, it can sometimes erode the sense of community.

This kind of stealthy use of technology is not limited to routing phone calls. The speed and lack of warning with which technology is introduced in public locations gives people little help with the transition. Without orientation or warning, one's sense of safety can be undermined, leading to a feeling of helplessness. When familiar systems in the community change in incomprehensible ways, people feel uncomfortable in what were once comfortable surroundings. The confusion caused by the introduction of new techno-faucets and gas pumps in our town are good examples of this increasingly common phenomenon.

Traditional community relationships between residents and local merchants were built on trust over time. In the past, the druggist knew his customers by name. The banker proudly showed off pictures of her grandchildren. These relationships have eroded in the face of technologically driven commerce. Inventory-management technology and automated manufacturing plants have allowed large merchandisers to undercut local merchants. The Home Shopping Network, cash machines, and Internet commerce have changed the way people do business. As a result, many people are feeling a loss of community.

Then, there is parity TechnoStress, caused by the fact that not everyone is "wired." Not all people know how to use technology or can afford to have very much of it in their homes, schools, or offices. We think of these two very different groups as the "Knows" and the "Know-Nots."

People who use technology in their jobs earn substantially more money. Those without technology will continue to fall further and further behind. Know-Nots recognize this. They are frightened because their jobs may be threatened or they cannot advance. But they also feel frustrated, distrustful, and alienated. They can't help but feel unequal. Technology has led to another unnecessary negative stratification in our society.

There are also huge differences in the use of technology based on geographic locations, ethnic background, gender, and family composition. A large chunk of society remains technologically out of the loop.

So, when it comes to technology, people are not created equal. What about other basic rights, such as privacy? Are they the same when technology is involved? Today, everything is computerized. Call to order something from a catalog you have used before, and the salesperson immediately sees a screen full of information about you. "Wouldn't you like to buy a jacket to go with the skis you bought last year?" You might wonder how he knew that. Try to buy a car and the dealer will check your credit. Have you looked at your credit report lately? You would be amazed at how much information it contains about your personal life and financial transactions. Many people worry about their privacy because of the widespread use of computers and the proliferation of databases and exchanged information.

Computers are routinely used to identify individual's buying patterns through credit card purchases. Appropriately matched catalogs soon show up in the mail. A simple box costing less than $30 can tap into cellular phone conversations. But it is even easier than that to use the telephone to invade someone's privacy. Telephone companies now allow anyone with a caller ID box to gain your telephone number, unless you take the responsibility to block that access. Many services on the Internet also list home addresses and telephone numbers. Technology has made the concept of individual privacy a thing of the past.

E-mail is not private; such messages can be intercepted and copied without leaving a trace. Your privacy is not even insured when you surf the Net. Every time you visit a Web site you leave a trail that tells people you were there, how long you stayed, and what you found interesting enough to pursue. Many programs that help you surf the Net leave what are called "cookies" on your own computer, which are essentially lists of sites you have visited. These nonedibles can be used to track your travels.

Perhaps most disconcerting of all is the fact that technology has opened up new mediums for assault—intentional and otherwise. A study by Ernst and Young found that 8 out of 10 North American companies lost valuable information to computer viruses and hackers. A virus is an unwanted set of commands that can enter your computer in a variety of ways. Viruses are sometimes deliberately sent to computer systems. It has become imperative for companies to use software designed to keep their computers virus-free. Viruses have even turned up on factory-sealed programs. Scores of new viruses are identified every month, and individual PCs are as prone to getting them as are large computer systems.

But viruses aren't the only problem compounding victimization by technology. Something as innocuous as e-mail can lead to you receiving thousand of pieces of electronic junk mail.

Global TechnoStress

Communication dodging, loss of privacy, and electronic victimization are TechnoStressors that impact people around the globe. In the early 1990s, we embarked on a massive undertaking—assessing the world's view of technology. With the help of colleagues around the globe, we collected data from over 3,500 university students in 23 countries. We found that countries could be placed into groups based on two factors: (1) how much technology their citizens used and (2) their attitudes toward technology. Some countries, such as India, Poland, and Indonesia, had little technological experience and tremendous technological discomfort. Others, such as Israel and Singapore, had a great deal of experience and very little discomfort. The rest fell into clearly defined pockets.

Western European nations had moderate experience and moderate-to-little discomfort. Third World nations mostly had very little technological sophistication and moderate discomfort.

The United States was neither the most technologically sophisticated country nor the most comfortable with modern technology. That place of honor was shared by Singapore and Israel. Before we embarked on this study, we had expected that Japan would be a member of this select group, too. However, we were surprised to find that 60% of more than 400 students from three Japanese universities were highly technophobic! This result became much less surprising when our further research revealed that, at that time, Japanese students had limited exposure to computers in school and at home due to political and cultural considerations. Students were suffering great TechnoStress when they entered the university.

Even in places where they are exposed to computers, people are not necessarily able to enjoy all the benefits. For example, Internet access in Europe and Asia is lagging far behind the United States. Many governments are struggling to control the flow of information to their citizens through censorship.

Ending Societal TechnoStress

Sven Birkerts, philosopher and author of *The Gutenberg Elegies: The Fate of Reading in an Electronic Age,* a book that criticizes modern technology, observed the following:

There seems to be this tremendous kind of shoulder-shrugging. You can't fight city hall about this one because it is being introduced from the upper institutional level on down. At a corporate level, you have no choice—you must be on-line. It's also moving rapidly into the schools. While this is not necessarily tragic, neither is it a matter of choice. We have not had a chance to debate this new technology in the way television got debated in our culture for a good decade in its early years.

Although people in general have had little to say about this explosion of technology, they can take positive steps to overcome societal TechnoStress:

1. *Develop an attitude that empowers you.* Believe in yourself as an agent of change, and clearly envision the goal of a more cohesive, safer society.
2. *Don't hide your TechnoStress. Let it show.* When stumped by technology, don't just walk away. Ask for help. This is a way to connect with another human being. With their assistance, you'll either master the new equipment or learn something by trying. At the very least, you'll be less intimidated by inevitable technological difficulties.
3. *Reach out to others struggling with technology.* If you have mastered a particular type of technology, help others. Share your trial-and-error learning experiences. You will feel reconnected, while helping to overcome someone else's confusion. And by teaching others, you will reinforce your own knowledge and perhaps even expand it.

4. *Make the impersonal personal.* Voice mail messages often say that holding for an operator is an option reserved only for people with rotary phones. But if a system offers you the option of pressing "0" for an operator, use it. You are entitled to real contact! When you call a toll-free number, and if you don't know where you have been routed, ask the person's name and where they are located. You might say something to make the conversation more personal, such as asking about the weather. This may make the person at the other end feel more connected to you. You'll probably get better service, too. Remember, people taking those calls sit in front of computers all day and also feel alienated. Work at making person-to-person contact, even if a system seems designed for person-to-technology communication.

5. *Be involved in technology's introduction into your community.* Don't stand by and watch technology show up in schools, libraries, and community centers without having a say. Be proactive. Find out who is in charge and offer to help. Attend meetings. Ask your civic leaders about technology plans for the community. Demand thorough attention to all aspects of a plan, including ongoing support. Help your community anticipate problems. A small town in the Midwest was planning to place computer terminals with free Internet access in all libraries and city buildings. The planners asked us about what problems people might have with the new terminals and we were able to design a straightforward way of introducing the program before the computers were installed. With this bit of advance

planning, the program was so successful that the town received a government grant for additional computers and to teach community computer classes.

A Better Future

People can make a difference in their personal lives and in society by challenging educators, politicians, local, state, and national agencies, marketers, developers, and business leaders to help eliminate the causes of TechnoStress. Throughout this book we have conveyed three important messages:

1. **You are not alone in your concern, discomfort, and fear of modern technology.**
2. **You are not the only one who has a difficult time learning to use technology.**
3. **You can overcome TechnoStress and make technology work for you.**

Your first step toward achieving techno-comfort is to become aware of how technology can affect you. As you use the tips in this book, you will feel decidedly better about technology and yourself. Your confidence and self-esteem will be enhanced. TechnoStress can be ousted from your life. And without it, you will be better prepared to take charge of and enjoy the technology of today and the changes that are coming tomorrow.

Selected Readings

< < < < < < < > > > > > > >

Chapter 1

Brod, Craig. *Technostress: The Human Cost of the Computer Revolution*. Reading, Mass.: Addison-Wesley, 1984.

Clark, Don, and Kyle Pope. "Poll Finds Americans Like Using PCs but May Find Them to Be Stressful." *Wall Street Journal,* 10 April 1995.

Henderson, Bill, ed. *Minutes of the Lead Pencil Club*. Wainscott, New York: Pushcart Press, 1996.

Jay, Timothy. "Computerphobia: What to Do about It." *Educational Technology* 21 (1981):47–48.

Lee, Robert. "Social Attitudes and the Computer Revolution." *Public Opinion Quarterly* 34–35 (1970):3–59.

Macaulay, David. *The Way Things Work.* Boston: Houghton-Mifflin, 1988.

Naisbitt, John. *Megatrends*. New York: Warner Books, 1982.

Norman, Donald A. *The Design of Everyday Things*. New York: Basic Books, 1988.

Rosen, Larry D., Deborah C. Sears, and Michelle M. Weil. "Computerphobia." *Behavior Research Methods, Instrumentation, and Computers* 19, no. 2. (1987):167–179.

———. "Treating Technophobia: A Longitudinal Evaluation of the Computerphobia Reduction Program." *Computers in Human Behavior* 9 (1993):27–50.

Rosen, Larry D., and Michelle M. Weil. "Adult and Teenage Consumer Users of Technology: Potholes on the Information Superhighway?" *Journal of Consumer Affairs* 29, no. 1. (1995):55–84.

———. "Easing the Transition from Paper to Computer-Based Systems." In *The Computerization of Behavioral Healthcare*, edited by T. Trabin. San Francisco: Jossey-Bass, 1996.

———. *The Mental Health Technology Bible*. New York: John Wiley & Sons, 1997.

Sale, Kirkpatrick. *Rebels against the Future*. Reading, Mass.: Addison-Wesley, 1995.

Stoll, Clifford. *Silicon Snake Oil*. New York: Doubleday, 1995.

Talbott, Stephen. *The Future Does Not Compute*. Sebastopol, Calif.: O'Reilly & Associates, 1985.

Taylor, Humphrey. *Awareness of Information Superhighway Grows but Knowledge and Understanding of Computing and Communications Still Patchy*. New York: Louis Harris & Associates, 1994.

Times Mirror Center for the People and the Press. *Technology in the American Household.* Washington, D.C.: Times Mirror, 1994.

Weil, Michelle M. *CyberSource: Cyber-Basics for Business People.* Atlanta, Ga.: networkMCl, 1995.

———. *Rx for the Techno-Phobic.* Arlington, Va.: MCI One, 1997.

Weil, Michelle M., Larry D. Rosen, and Stuart Wugalter. "The Etiology of Computerphobia." *Computers in Human Behavior* 6 (1990):361–379.

Chapter 2

Dunn, Rita, and Shirley Griggs. *Learning Styles: Quiet Revolution in American Secondary Schools.* Reston, Va.: National Association of Secondary School Principals, 1988.

———. *Multiculturalism and Learning Styles: Teaching and Counseling Adolescents.* Westport, Conn.: Praeger, 1995.

Harmon, Amy. "Earfuls of High-Tech Horrors." *Los Angeles Times,* 30 December 1996.

Keefe, James, and John Monk. *Learning Style Profile.* Reston, Va.: National Association of Secondary School Principals, 1988.

Miller, George. "The Magical Number Seven, Plus or Minus Two: Some Limits on Our Capacity for Processing Information." *Psychological Review* 63 (1956): 81–97.

Miller, Greg. "Don't Call Us." *Los Angeles Times,* 29 April 1996.

Norman, Donald A. *The Design of Everyday Things*. New York: Basic Books, 1988.

———. *Turn Signals Are the Facial Expressions of Automobiles*. Reading, Mass.: Addison-Wesley, 1992.

———. *Things That Make Us Smart*. Reading, Mass.: Addison-Wesley, 1993.

Rimm, Deborah C., and J. C. Masters. *Behavior Therapy*. New York: Academic Press, 1979.

Rosen, Larry D., and Michelle M. Weil. "Easing the Transition from Paper to Computer-Based Systems." In *The Computerization of Behavioral Healthcare,* edited by T. Trabin. San Francisco: Jossey-Bass, 1996.

———. *Study 3: Public Interest on the Information Superhighway*. 1996. http://www.csudh.edu/psych/study3 .htm; INTERNET.

Weil, Michelle M., and Larry D. Rosen. *Study 2: Comparison of Online Users and Nonusers*. 1996. http:// www.csudh.edu/psych/study2x.htm; INTERNET.

Chapter 3

Baron, Robert. "The Sweet Smell of . . . Helping: Effects of Pleasant Ambient Fragrance on Prosocial Behavior in Shopping Malls." *Personality and Social Psychology Bulletin,* in press.

Blanck, Gertrude, and Rubin Blanck. *Ego Psychology: Theory and Practice*. New York: Columbia University Press, 1974.

Bowlby, John. 1969. *Attachment*. New York: Basic Books, 1969.

Goldberg, Arnold. *Progress in Self Psychology*. New York: Guilford Press, 1985.

Lax, Ruth, Sheldon Bach, and J. Alexis Burland. *Rapprochement: The Critical Subphase of Separation Individuation*. New York: Jason Aronson, 1980.

Mahler, Margaret. *Infantile Psychosis and Early Contributions*. Vol. 1 of *The Selected Papers of Margaret S. Mahler, M.D.* New York: Jason Aronson, 1979.

Rotton, J., and S. White. "Air Pollution, the Sick Building Syndrome, and Social Behavior." *Environmental International* 22, no. 1. (1996):53–60.

Scott, Anne. "A Beginning Theory of Personal Space Boundaries." *Perspectives in Psychiatric Care* 29, no. 2. (1993):12–21.

Chapter 4

Blanck, Rubin, and Gertrude Blanck. *Beyond Ego Psychology: Developmental Object Relations Theory*. New York: Columbia University Press, 1986.

Bloom, Lois. *The Transition from Infancy to Language: Acquiring the Power of Expression*. New York: Cambridge University Press, 1993.

Bowie, Malcolm. *Psychoanalysis and the Future of Theory*. London: Blackwell, 1994.

Bruner, Jerome. *Child's Talk: Learning to Use Language*. New York: W. W. Norton, 1985.

Cairns, Helen Smith. *The Acquisition of Language*. 2nd ed. Austin, Tex.: Pro-Ed, 1996.

Goldberg, Arnold. *A Fresh Look at Psychoanalysis: The View from Self Psychology*. Hillsdale, N.J.: Analytic Press, 1988.

Howard, Merle, and Lloyd Hulit. *Born to Talk: An Introduction to Speech and Language Development*. Boston: Allyn & Bacon, 1996.

Martin, Judith. *Miss Manners' Basic Training: Communication*. New York: Crown, 1997.

Turkle, Sherry. *The Second Self: Computers and the Human Spirit*. New York: Simon & Schuster, 1984.

———. *Life on the Screen*. New York: Simon & Schuster, 1995.

Weil, Michelle M. "From the Couch to Cyber-Therapy." *The National Psychologist* 5, no. 5:1B–4B, 1996.

Chapter 5

Anderson, John R. *Learning and Memory: An Integrated Approach*. New York: John Wiley & Sons, 1995.

———. *The Architecture of Cognition*. Hillsdale, N.J.: Lawrence Erlbaum Associates, 1996.

Coren, Stanley. *Sleep Thieves*. New York: Free Press, 1996.

Gooddy, William. *Time and the Nervous System*. Westport, Conn.: Praeger, 1988.

Hassoun, Mohamad. *Associative Neural Memories: Theory and Implementation*. New York: Oxford University Press, 1993.

McClelland, James, and David Rumelhart. *Parallel Distributed Processing: Explorations in the Microstructure of Cognition*. Boston: Bradford Book, 1988.

McGrath, Joseph. *The Social Psychology of Time*. Newbury Park, Calif.: Sage, 1988.

Rechtschaffen, Stephan. *Time Shifting*. New York: Doubleday, 1996.

Toffler, Alvin. *The Third Wave*. New York: William Morrow, 1980.

———. *Power Shift*. New York: Bantam Books, 1990.

Chapter 6

Classroom Connect. *Child Safety on the Internet*. New York: Prentice Hall, 1997.

Collis, Betty, Gerald Knezak, Kwok-Wing Lai, Keiko Miyashita, Willem Pelgrum, Tjeerd Plomp, and Takashi Sakamoto. *Children and Computers in School*. Hillsdale, N.J.: Lawrence Erlbaum Associates, 1996.

Hiltz, Starr Roxanne. *The Virtual Classroom*. Norwood N.J.: Ablex Publishing, 1994.

Kerr, Michael, and Murray Bowen. *Family Evaluation: An Approach Based on Bowen Theory*. New York: W. W. Norton, 1988.

L'Abate, Luciano. *Handbook of Developmental Family Psychology and Psychopathology*. New York: John Wiley & Sons, 1989.

National Center for Education Statistics. *Digest of Education Statistics, 1995.* http://www.ed.gov/NCES/pubs/D95; INTERNET.

National Center for Missing and Exploited Children. *Child Safety on the Information Highway.* Arlington, Va.: National Center for Missing and Exploited Children, 1994.

Papero, David. *Bowen Family System Therapy.* Boston: Allyn & Bacon, 1990.

Pipher, Mary. *The Shelter of Each Other.* New York: Grosset/Putnam, 1996.

Rocheleau, Bruce. "Computer Use by School-Age Children: Trends, Patterns and Predictors." *Journal of Educational Computing Research,* 12, no. 1. (1995):1–17.

Sussman, Marvin. *Personal Computers and the Family.* New York: Haworth Press, 1985.

The Children's Partnership. *Children and New Technologies.* 1996. http://www.childrenspartnership.org/americaschild; INTERNET.

Times Mirror Center for the People and the Press. *Technology in the American Household.* Washington, D.C.: Times Mirror, 1994.

Wolff, Michael. *Where We Stand.* New York: Bantam, 1992.

Chapter 7

Meade, Jeff. *Home Sweet Office: The Ultimate Out-of-Office Experience.* Princeton, N.J.: Peterson's Guides, 1993.

Pratt, Joanne. *Myths and Realities of Working at Home.* Small Business Administration, 1993.

Sutton, David and Paul Sims. *MCl-Gallup Study: Small Business Bullish on Cyberspace.* [Press Release] Washington, D.C.: MCl Business Markets, 1995.

Telecommute America! http://www.att.com/Telecommute _America; INTERNET.

U.S. Small Business Administration. http://www.sba.gov; INTERNET.

Chapter 8

Champy, James. *Fast Forward: The Best Ideas on Managing Business Change.* Boston: Harvard Business School Press, 1996.

Davidow, William, and Michael Melon. *The Virtual Corporation.* New York: HarperBusiness, 1992.

U.S. Chamber of Commerce. *U.S. Chamber of Commerce Telecommunications Infrastructure Task Force: Report of Findings of the National Information Infrastructure Survey.* 1995.

Finley, Michael. *Techno-Crazed.* Pace-Setter Books, 1995.

Garson, Barbara. *The Electronic Sweatshop.* New York: Simon & Schuster, 1988.

Harp, Candice. "IS Training for Less." *Computerworld,* 12 October 1996.

Igbaria, Magid, Stephen Schiffman, and Thomas Wieckowski. "The Respective Roles of Perceived Fun in the Acceptance of Microcomputer Technology." *Behaviour and Information Technology* 13, no. 6. (1994):349–361.

Landauer, Thomas. *The Trouble with Computers.* Boston: MIT Press, 1995.

Moore, Geoffrey. *Inside the Tornado*. New York: Harper-Business, 1995.

Rifkin, Jeremy. *The End of Work: The Decline of the Global Labor Force and the Dawn of the Post-Market Era*. New York: Tarcher/Putnam, 1995.

Rosen, Larry D., and Michelle M. Weil. "Easing the Transition from Paper to Computer-Based Systems." In *The Computerization of Behavioral Healthcare,* edited by T. Trabin. San Francisco: Jossey-Bass, 1996.

———. *Study 1: Business Technology Use*. 1996. http://www.csudh.edu/psych/study1x.htm; INTERNET.

Sethi, Amarjit, Denis Caro, and Randall Schuler. *Strategic Management of Technostress in an Information Society*. Lewiston, N.Y.: Hogrefe, 1987.

Shenk, David. *Data Smog: Surviving the Information Glut*. San Francisco: HarperEdge, 1997.

Zuboff, Shoshana. *In the Age of the Smart Machine*. New York: Basic Books, 1988.

Chapter 9

Birkerts, Sven. *The Gutenberg Elegies: The Fate of Reading in an Electronic Age*. New York: Fawcett-Columbine, 1994.

Classroom Connect. *Child Safety on the Internet*. New York: Prentice Hall, 1997.

Ellul, Jacques. *The Technological Bluff*. Grand Rapids, Mich.: Eerdmans Publishing, 1990.

Gates, Bill. *The Road Ahead*. New York: Viking-Penguin, 1995.

Hafner, Katie, and John Markoff. *Cyberpunk*. New York: Simon & Schuster, 1991.

Hardison, O. B. *Disappearing through the Skylight*. New York: Viking, 1989.

Naisbitt, John. *Megatrends*. New York: Warner Books, 1982.

———. *Global Paradox*. New York: William Morrow, 1994.

Negroponte, Nicholas. *Being Digital*. New York: Alfred A. Knopf, 1995.

Rosenberger, Rob. *Computer Virus Myths*. http://kumite.com/myths; INTERNET.

Roszak, Theodore. *The Cult of Information*. New York: Pantheon, 1986.

Teich, Albert. *Technology and the Future*. 7th ed. New York: St. Martin's Press, 1997.

Tenner, Edward. *Why Things Bite Back*. New York: Alfred A. Knopf, 1996.

Volti, Rudy. *Society and Technological Change*. 3rd ed. New York: St. Martin's Press, 1995.

Weil, Michelle M., and Larry D. Rosen. "The Psychological Impact of Technology from a Global Perspective: A Study of Technological Sophistication and Technophobia in University Students from 23 Countries." *Computers in Human Behavior* 11, no. 11. (1995): 95–133.

Wurman, Richard Saul. *Information Anxiety*. New York: Doubleday, 1989.

Index

‹ ‹ ‹ ‹ ‹ ‹ ‹ › › › › › › ›

‹ Index ›

Creativity, techno-facade of, 162–164

Credit reports, privacy issues for, 214

D

Design of Everyday Things, The (Norman), 22–23, 32

Deskilling, 193

Dyads, 132–134

E

Eager Adopters, 17–18
  common reactions from, 21
  in corporations, 178, 182, 184
  increasing awareness and support skills of, 196–198
  learning approach of, 46–47
  percentage of, 22
  as teachers, 36, 45

Ego. *See* On-line ego

Electronic communications, 71–72, 96–97
  developing on-line ego, 94–96
  etiquette of, 79–81
  evolution of, 73–74
  incompletion vs. completion, 86–91
  K.I.S.S. Principle, 81–83
  privacy issues for, 213–214
  See also On-line communications

Electronic Privacy Act of 1986, 178

Electronic surveillance, 178–179

E-mail. *See* Electronic communications; On-line communications

Emergency Techno-Crash Plan (ETCP), 169–171

Emoticons, 85–86

Emotional learning elements, 39–40

End of Work, The (Rifkin), 177–178

Environmental learning elements, 38

External structure, vs. internal structure, 40

F

Family, 125–126
  balance between togetherness and separateness, 132–134
  continued growth of, 136–137
  rules of, 135–136
  technological interference in, 137–142
  technological isolation of, 127–132
  See also Techno-family system

Family homeostasis, 134–135

Family Pow-Wow, 150

Family Systems Theory, 132–137

Fast Forward (Champy), 181

‹ Index ›

K

Kinesthetic learning
channels. *See* Tactile
learning channels
K.I.S.S. Principle, 81–83

L

Landauer, Thomas, *The
Trouble with Computers,*
198
Lead Pencil Club, 23–24
Learning
difficulties in, 35–37
narrowing focus of, 47–48
successful strategy for,
46–47
Learning channels, 41–42, 44
Learning environment, 42–43
Learning process, 43–45
Learning styles, 37–38
emotional elements, 39–40
environmental elements,
38
physical elements, 41–42
social elements, 40
Lee, Robert, 10
Long-term memory, 28, 31

M

Machine Machismo, 64–66
Megatrends (Naisbitt), 8
Memory
and Multitasking Madness,
111, 112–113
sensory, short-term, and
long-term, 28–31
Mental schemata, 34
Minute Minders, 122

Modality Matching, 88
Moore's Law, 207
Motivation, 39, 194–196
Motorola's Guide to
Productive
Telecommuting,
161–162
Multitasking Madness,
107–115, 167

N

Naisbitt, John, *Megatrends,* 8
National Association of
Music Merchants, 159
National Center for Missing
and Exploited Children,
*Child Safety on the
Information Highway,*
149
Neo-Luddites, 24
Netiquette, 144
Norman, Donald
*Design of Everyday Things,
The,* 22–23, 32
*Things That Make Us
Smart,* 32
*Turn Signals Are the
Facial Expressions of
Automobiles,* 32

O

On-line communications,
91–94
children's access to,
141–142
family rules for, 146–150
and Netiquette, 144
On-line ego, 94–96

237